Burns and Oates

The Daily Prayer-Book

Compiled From Various Sources

Burns and Oates

The Daily Prayer-Book
Compiled From Various Sources

ISBN/EAN: 9783741190537

Manufactured in Europe, USA, Canada, Australia, Japa

Cover: Foto ©Lupo / pixelio.de

Manufactured and distributed by brebook publishing software (www.brebook.com)

Burns and Oates

The Daily Prayer-Book

THE
DAILY PRAYER-BOOK.

COMPILED FROM VARIOUS SOURCES.

"Oratio justi clavis est cœli; ascendit precatio et descendit Dei miseratio."

"The prayer of the just man is the key of Heaven; even as his prayer goes up the mercy of God comes down."
ST. AUGUSTINE.

LONDON:
BURNS & OATES.

NIHIL OBSTAT.

RICARDUS M. STANTON,
CONG. ORAT. PRESB. CENSOR DEPUTATUS.

Die 17 *Octobris,* 1881.

IMPRIMATUR.

HENRICUS EDUARDUS,
CARD. ARCHIEP. WESTMON.

The Daily Prayer - Book is intended to provide short forms of prayers for ordinary use. The contents have been compiled from various sources, especially from *The Treasury of Prayer.*

CONTENTS.

	PAGE
Acts of Faith, Hope, Charity, and Contrition	14
Angelus	17
Asperges	40
Anima Christi	126
Ave Verum	126
Ave Maris Stella	182
Before and After Communion	129
Benediction of Blessed Sacrament	106
Blessed Sacrament, Visit to	137
Commandments, The Ten	5
" of the Church	5
Confiteor	12
Confession	112
Communion	124
Corporal Works of Mercy	7
Creed, The Apostles'	10
Crucifix, Indulgenced, Prayer before	128
Daily Meditation	9
Daily Exercises	25
Days of Obligation and Devotion	2
Deadly Sins	8
Death, Prayers for Happy	144
De Profundis	20
Divine Praises	24

Contents.

	PAGE
Dolours, The Seven, Chaplet of	179
Dying, Prayers for	149
Evening Prayers	34
Grace at Meals	13
Holy Souls, Prayers for	91
Itinerarium	139
Lay Baptism	15
Litany of the Holy Name	30
" of the Blessed Virgin	35
" of the Saints	154
Mass, Ordinary	43
" Prayers at	80
" Blessed Leonard's Method for	92
" Serving at	100
Morning Prayers	27
Miserere	150
Nunc Dimittis	39
Regina Cœli	18
Rosary, The	178
Sacraments, The	6
Salve Regina	22
Sickness, Prayers in	136
Sick, Prayer for the	136
Te Deum	184
Various Prayers	130
Veni, Creator	180
Viaticum, Holy	147

TABLE OF MOVEABLE FEASTS.

Year of our Lord.	Ash Wednesday.	Easter Sunday.	Ascension Day.	Whit-Sunday.	Corpus Christi.	First Sunday in Advent.
1881	Mar. 2	Apr. 17	May 26	June 5	June 16	Nov. 27
1882	Feb. 22	Apr. 9	May 18	May 28	June 8	Dec. 3
1883	Feb. 7	Mar. 25	May 3	May 13	May 24	Dec. 2
1884	Feb. 27	Apr. 13	May 22	June 1	June 12	Nov. 30
1885	Feb. 18	Apr. 5	May 14	May 24	June 4	Nov. 29
1886	Mar. 10	Apr. 25	June 3	June 13	June 24	Nov. 28
1887	Feb. 23	Apr. 10	May 19	May 29	June 9	Nov. 27
1888	Feb. 15	Apr. 1	May 10	May 20	May 31	Dec. 2
1889	Mar. 6	Apr. 21	May 30	June 9	June 20	Dec. 1
1890	Feb. 19	Apr. 6	May 15	May 25	June 5	Nov. 30
1891	Feb. 11	Mar. 29	May 7	May 17	May 28	Nov. 29
1892	Mar. 2	Apr. 17	May 26	June 5	June 16	Nov. 27
1893	Feb. 15	Apr. 2	May 11	May 21	June 1	Dec. 3
1894	Feb. 7	Mar. 25	May 3	May 13	May 24	Dec. 2
1895	Feb. 27	Apr. 14	May 23	June 2	June 13	Dec. 1
1896	Feb. 19	Apr. 5	May 14	May 24	June 4	Nov. 29
1897	Mar. 3	Apr. 18	May 27	June 6	June 17	Nov. 28
1898	Feb. 23	Apr. 10	May 19	May 29	June 9	Nov. 27
1899	Feb. 15	Apr. 2	May 11	May 21	June 1	Dec. 3
1900	Feb. 28	Apr. 15	May 24	June 3	June 14	Dec. 2
1901	Feb. 20	Apr. 7	May 16	May 26	June 6	Dec. 1

The Ecclesiastical Year, with regard to the Sundays and Moveable Feasts, begins with Advent. The words *Double*, *Semi-double*, and *Simple*, show the degrees of solemnity with which the Offices of the Church are celebrated. The principal Festivals are *Doubles of the first class*. Some Festivals have an Octave, or succession of eight days, on which, with certain exceptions, the Office and Mass of the Feast are said. A *Feria* is a week-day for which no Saint's Office is appointed. When the Office is *double*, an entire Antiphon is said or sung before and after each Psalm; when *semi-double* or *simple*, only a word or two are said or sung before the Psalm.

A TABLE

Of all the Feasts observed in England with an obligation of hearing Mass and resting from servile work.

All Sundays in the year.

JANUARY	1	The Circumcision of our Lord, or New Year's Day.
	6	The Epiphany, or Twelfth Day.
JUNE	29	St. Peter and St. Paul, Apostles.
AUGUST	15	The Assumption of the Blessed Virgin Mary.
NOVEMBER	1	All Saints.
DECEMBER	25	Christmas Day.

Ascension-day.
Corpus Christi (being 1st Thursday after Trinity Sunday).

In Scotland:
NOVEMBER 30 St. Andrew, Apostle.

In Ireland:
MARCH 17 St. Patrick, Apostle.
25 Annunciation B. V. M.

DAYS OF DEVOTION.
(Formerly Festivals of Obligation.)

FEBRUARY 2 The Purification, or Candlemas Day.
24 St. Matthias, Apostle.

MARCH	19	St. Joseph, Spouse of the Blessed Virgin.
	25	The Annunciation of the B. V., or Lady-day.
APRIL	23	St. George the Martyr.
MAY	1	St. Philip and St. James, Apostles.
	3	The Finding of the Cross.
JUNE	24	The Nativity of St. John Baptist.
JULY	25	St. James, Apostle.
	26	St. Anne, Mother of the Blessed Virgin.
AUGUST	10	St. Laurence, Martyr.
	24	St. Bartholomew, Apostle.
SEPTEMBER	8	The Nativity of the Blessed Virgin.
	21	St. Matthew, Apostle.
	29	Michaelmas Day.
OCTOBER	28	St. Simon and St. Jude, Apostles.
NOVEMBER	30	St. Andrew, Apostle.
DECEMBER	8	The Immaculate Conception of the Blessed Virgin.
	21	St. Thomas, Apostle.
	26	St. Stephen, Martyr.
	27	St. John, Apostle.
	28	Holy Innocents.
	29	St. Thomas of Canterbury.
	31	St. Silvester.

Easter Monday and Tuesday.
Monday and Tuesday in Whitsun-week.

FASTING DAYS.

All the week-days of *Lent*, beginning on *Ash Wednesday*.
The *Wednesdays* and *Fridays* in *Advent*.
Ember-days, four times a year—viz., the *Wednesdays*, *Fridays*, and *Saturdays*—
    1. Next after the first Sunday in *Lent;*
    2. In *Whitsun week;*
    3. Next after the 14th of *September;*
    4. Next after the third Sunday of *Advent*.
The *Vigil* of SS. *Peter* and *Paul, June* 28.
The *Vigil* of the *Assumption, August* 14.
The *Vigil* of *All Saints, October* 31.
The *Vigil* of the *Nativity* of our Lord, *December* 24.
The *Vigil* of *Pentecost*.

DAYS OF ABSTINENCE.

All *Fridays*, except *Christmas-day* when it falls on a Friday.
The Sundays in Lent unless a dispensation be granted.
The solemnities of *Marriage* are forbidden from the first *Sunday* in *Advent* until after *Twelfth-day*, and from *Ash-Wednesday* until *Low-Sunday*.

CHRISTIAN DOCTRINE.

The Ten Commandments of God.

1. Thou shalt not have strange gods before me. Thou shalt not make to thyself any graven thing, nor the likeness of anything that is in heaven above or in the earth beneath, nor of those things that are in the waters under the earth: Thou shalt not adore them nor serve them.
2. Thou shalt not take the name of the Lord thy God in vain.
3. Remember that thou keep holy the Sabbath-day.
4. Honour thy father and thy mother.
5. Thou shalt not kill.
6. Thou shalt not commit adultery.
7. Thou shalt not steal.
8. Thou shalt not bear false witness against thy neighbour.
9. Thou shalt not covet thy neighbour's wife.
10. Thou shalt not covet thy neighbour's goods.

The Six Commandments of the Church.

1. To keep certain days holy, with the obligation of resting from servile works.

2. To hear Mass on all Sundays and holidays of obligation.

3. To keep the days of fasting and abstinence appointed by the Church.

4. To go to Confession at least once a year.

5. To receive the Blessed Sacrament at least once a year, and that at Easter or thereabouts.

6. Not to marry within certain degrees of kindred, nor to solemnize marriage at the forbidden times.

The Seven Sacraments.

Baptism	*Matt.* xxviii. 19.
Confirmation . .	*Acts* viii. 17.
Holy Eucharist . .	*Matt.* xxvi. 26.
Penance	*John* xx. 23.
Extreme Unction .	*James* v. 14.
Holy Order . . .	*Luke* xxii. 19.
Matrimony . . .	*Matt.* xix. 6.

The Three Theological Virtues.

Faith—Hope—and Charity.

The Four Cardinal Virtues.

Prudence—Justice—Fortitude—and Temperance.

The Seven Gifts of the Holy Ghost.—Isa. xi. 2, 3.

Wisdom,	Knowledge,
Understanding,	Piety, and
Counsel,	The Fear of the
Fortitude,	Lord.

The Corporal Works of Mercy.

To feed the hungry,
To give drink to the thirsty,
To clothe the naked,
To harbour the harbourless,
To visit the sick,
To visit the captive, and
To bury the dead.

The Spiritual Works of Mercy.

To convert the sinner,
To instruct the ignorant,
To counsel the doubtful,
To comfort the sorrowful,
To bear wrongs patiently,
To forgive injuries,
To pray for the living and the dead.

The Eight Beatitudes.—Matt. v.

1. Blessed are the poor in spirit; for theirs is the kingdom of heaven.
2. Blessed are the meek; for they shall possess the land.
3. Blessed are they that mourn; for they shall be comforted.
4. Blessed are they that hunger and thirst after justice; for they shall have their fill.
5. Blessed are the merciful; for they shall obtain mercy.
6. Blessed are the clean of heart; for they shall see God.
7. Blessed are the peacemakers; for they shall be called the children of God.

8. Blessed are they that suffer persecution for justice' sake; for theirs is the kingdom of heaven.

The Seven Deadly Sins, and the opposite Virtues

Pride,	*Contrary Virtues.*	Humility.
Covetousness,		Liberality.
Lust,		Chastity.
Anger,		Meekness.
Gluttony,		Temperance.
Envy,		Brotherly love.
Sloth,		Diligence.

Sins against the Holy Ghost.

Presumption of God's mercy—Despair—Resisting the known truth—Envy at another's spiritual good—Obstinacy in sin—Final impenitence.

Sins crying to Heaven for Vengeance.

Wilful murder—The sin of Sodom—Oppression of the poor—Defrauding labourers of their wages.

Nine Ways of being Accessory to another's Sin.

By counsel—By command—By consent—By provocation—By praise or flattery—By concealment—By partaking—By silence—By defence of the ill done.

Three Eminent Good Works.

Prayer—Fasting—and Alms-deeds.

The Evangelical Counsels.

Voluntary Poverty—Perpetual Chastity—and Entire Obedience.

The four last Things to be remembered.

Death—Judgment—Hell—and Heaven.

Subjects for Daily Meditation.

Remember, Christian soul, that thou hast this day, and every day of thy life,—

God to glorify,
Jesus to imitate,
The Angels and Saints to invoke,
A soul to save,
A body to mortify,
Sins to expiate,
Virtues to acquire,
Hell to avoid,
Heaven to gain,
Eternity to prepare for,
Time to profit by,
Neighbours to edify,
The world to despise,
Devils to combat,
Passions to subdue,
Death perhaps to suffer,
And Judgment to undergo.

PATER NOSTER.

Pater noster, qui es in cœlis, sanctificetur nomen tuum: adveniat regnum tuum; fiat voluntas tua, sicut in cœlo et in terra. Panem nostrum quotidianum da nobis hodie: et dimitte nobis debita nostra, sicut et nos dimittimus debitoribus nostris: et ne nos inducas in tentationem; sed libera nos a malo. Amen.

AVE MARIA.

Ave Maria, gratia plena, Dominus tecum: benedicta tu in mulieribus, et benedictus fructus ventris tui, Jesus. Sancta Maria, Mater Dei, ora pro nobis peccatoribus, nunc et in hora mortis nostræ. Amen.

CREDO.

Credo in Deum, Patrem omnipotentem, Creatorem cœli et terræ. Et in Jesum Christum, Filium ejus unicum, Dominum nostrum; qui conceptus est de Spiritu Sancto, natus ex Maria Virgine, passus sub Pontio Pilato, crucifixus, mortuus, et sepultus; descendit ad inferos; tertia die resurrexit a mortuis; ascendit ad cœlos, sedet ad dexteram Dei Patris omnipotentis; inde venturus est judicare vivos et mortuos. Credo in Spiritum Sanctum, sanctam Ecclesiam Catholicam, Sanctorum communionem, remissionem peccatorum, carnis resurrectionem, vitam æternam. Amen.

OUR FATHER.

Our Father, who art in heaven, hallowed be Thy name: Thy kingdom come; Thy will be done on earth as it is in heaven. Give us this day our daily bread: and forgive us our trespasses, as we forgive them that trespass against us: and lead us not into temptation; but deliver us from evil. Amen.

HAIL MARY.

Hail Mary, full of grace; the Lord is with thee: blessed art thou amongst women, and blessed is the fruit of thy womb, Jesus. Holy Mary, Mother of God, pray for us sinners, now and at the hour of our death. Amen.

THE APOSTLES' CREED.

I believe in God the Father Almighty, Creator of heaven and earth. And in Jesus Christ, His only Son, our Lord; who was conceived by the Holy Ghost, born of the Virgin Mary, suffered under Pontius Pilate, was crucified, dead, and buried; He descended into hell; the third day He rose again from the dead; He ascended into heaven, sitteth at the right hand of God the Father Almighty; from thence He shall come to judge the living and the dead. I believe in the Holy Ghost, the Holy Catholic Church, the Communion of Saints, the forgiveness of sins, the resurrection of the body, and life everlasting. Amen.

CONFITEOR.

Confiteor Deo omnipotenti, beatæ Mariæ semper Virgini, beato Michaeli Archangelo, beato Joanni Baptistæ, sanctis Apostolis Petro et Paulo, *et* omnibus Sanctis (et tibi pater, *or*, vobis fratres), quia peccavi nimis cogitatione, verbo et opere, mea culpa, mea culpa, mea maxima culpa. Ideo precor beatam Mariam semper Virginem, beatum Michaelem Archangelum, beatum Joannem Baptistam, sanctos Apostolos Petrum et Paulum, *et* omnes Sanctos (et te pater, *or*, vos fratres), orare pro me ad Dominum Deum nostrum.

Misereatur nostri (tui *or* vestri) omnipotens Deus, et dimissis peccatis nostris (tuis *or* vestris) perducat nos (te *or* vos) ad vitam æternam. Amen.

Indulgentiam, absolutionem et remissionem peccatorum nostrorum tribuat nobis omnipotens et misericors Dominus. Amen.

BENEDICTIO MENSÆ ANTE PRANDIUM.

Benedic, Domine, nos et hæc tua dona, quæ de tua largitate sumus sumpturi; per Christum Dominum nostrum. Amen.

POST PRANDIUM.

Agimus tibi gratias, omnipotens Deus, pro universis beneficiis tuis: qui vivis et regnas in sæcula sæculorum. Amen.

Fidelium animæ, per misericordiam Dei, requiescant in pace. Amen.

CONFITEOR.

I confess to Almighty God, to blessed Mary ever Virgin, to blessed Michael the Archangel, to blessed John the Baptist, to the holy Apostles Peter and Paul, *and* to all the Saints (and to you, father, or you, brethren), that I have sinned exceedingly in thought, word, and deed: through my fault, through my fault, through my most grievous fault. Therefore, I beseech the blessed Mary ever Virgin, blessed Michael the Archangel, blessed John the Baptist, the holy Apostles Peter and Paul, *and* all the Saints (and you, father, or, you, brethren), to pray to the Lord our God for me.

May Almighty God have mercy upon us (thee or you), forgive us our sins, and bring us to life everlasting. Amen.

May the Almighty and merciful Lord grant us pardon, absolution, and remission of all our sins. Amen.

The words between brackets are omitted in private recitation.

GRACE BEFORE MEAT.

Bless us, O Lord, and these Thy gifts, which we are about to receive from Thy bounty. Through Christ our Lord. Amen.

GRACE AFTER MEAT.

We give Thee thanks, Almighty God, for all Thy benefits; who livest and reignest, world without end. Amen.

May the souls of the faithful, through the mercy of God, rest in peace. Amen.

ACTS OF FAITH, HOPE, CHARITY, AND CONTRITION.

AN ACT OF FAITH.

I firmly believe there is one God; and that in this one God there are Three Persons, the Father, the Son, and the Holy Ghost; that the Son took to Himself the nature of man, from the Virgin Mary's womb, by the power of the Holy Ghost; and that in this our human nature he was crucified and died for us; that afterwards he rose again and ascended into heaven, from thence he shall come to repay the just everlasting glory, and the wicked everlasting punishment; moreover, I believe whatsoever else the Catholic Church proposes to be believed, and this because God, who is the sovereign Truth, who can neither deceive nor be deceived, has revealed all these things to this His Church.

AN ACT OF HOPE.

O my God, relying on Thy almighty power and Thy infinite mercy and goodness, and because Thou art faithful to Thy promises, I trust in Thee that Thou wilt grant me forgiveness of my sins, through the merits of Jesus Christ, Thy Son; and that Thou wilt give me the assistance of Thy grace, with which I may labour to continue to the end in the diligent exercise of all good works, and may deserve to obtain the glory which Thou hast promised in Heaven.

AN ACT OF CHARITY.

O Lord, my God, I love Thee with my whole heart, and above all things, because Thou, O God, art the sovereign Good, and for Thy own infinite perfections, art most worthy of all love ; and for Thy sake, I also love my neighbour as myself.

AN ACT OF CONTRITION.

O my God, who art infinitely good, and always hatest sin, I beg pardon from my heart for all my offences against Thee. I detest them all, and am heartily sorrow for them ; because they offend Thy infinite goodness ; and I firmly resolve by the help of Thy grace never more to offend Thee, and carefully to avoid the occasions of sin.

LAY BAPTISM.

Provided an infant is in danger of dying before a Priest can be procured, any other person, whether man, woman, or child, may baptize it in the following manner :—

Whilst pouring common water on the head or face of the infant, pronounce the words,

" I baptize thee in the name of the Father, and of the Son, and of the Holy Ghost. Amen."

THE ANGELUS.

V. Angelus Domini nuntiavit Mariæ.
R. Et concepit de Spiritu Sancto.
Ave Maria.
V. Ecce ancilla Domini.
R. Fiat mihi secundum verbum tuum.
Ave Maria.
V. Et Verbum caro factum est.
R. Et habitavit in nobis.
Ave Maria.
V. Ora pro nobis, sancta Dei genitrix.
R. Ut digni efficiamur promissionibus Christi.

Oremus.

Gratiam tuam, quæsumus, Domine, mentibus nostris infunde; ut qui Angelo nuntiante Christi Filii tui incarnationem cognovimus, per Passionem ejus et Crucem ad resurrectionis gloriam perducamur. Per eumdem Christum Dominum nostrum. Amen.

Angelus dicitur flexis genibus præterquam in Dominicis, a primis vesperis, id est a vesperis Sabbati; et in tempore Paschali (a Sabbato Sancto usque ad Dominicum Trinitatis, quando dicitur stando.

THE ANGELUS.

V. The Angel of the Lord announced unto Mary.

R. And she conceived of the Holy Ghost.

Hail Mary.

V. Behold the handmaid of the Lord.

R. Be it done unto me according to Thy word.

Hail Mary.

V. And the Word was made flesh.

R. And dwelt among us.

Hail Mary.

N. Pray for us, O holy Mother of God.

R. That we may be made worthy of the promises of Christ.

Let us pray.

Pour forth, we beseech Thee, O Lord, Thy grace into our hearts, that we, to whom the Incarnation of Christ Thy Son was made known by the message of an Angel, may, by His Passion and Cross, be brought to the glory of His Resurrection, through the same Christ our Lord. Amen. [100 *days.*

The Angelus is said kneeling, except on Sundays, beginning with First Vespers, that is, Saturday evening; and in Paschal time (from Holy Saturday to Trinity Sunday), when it is said standing.

REGINA CŒLI.

A COMPLETORIO SABBATI SANCTI USQUE AD NONAM SABBATI POST PENTECOSTEN INCLUSIVE DICITUR ANTIPHONA.

Regina Cœli, lætare ! alleluia.
Quia quem meruisti portare : alleluia.
Resurrexit sicut dixit : alleluia.
Ora pro nobis Deum : alleluia.
V. Gaude et lætare, Virgo Maria : alleluia.
R. Quia surrexit Dominus vere : alleluia.

Oremus.

Deus, qui per resurrectionem Filii tui Domini nostri Jesu Christi mundum lætificare dignatus es; præsta, quæsumus, ut per ejus Genitricem Virginem Mariam perpetuæ capiamus gaudia vitæ. Per eumdem Christum Dominum nostrum. Amen.

GLORIA PATRI.

Gloria Patri et Filio et Spiritui Sancto. Sicut erat in principio, et nunc et semper et in sæcula sæculorum. Amen.

The indulgences attached to a single devout recital are given after each prayer : the others may be found in the Racoolta of Indulgences.

REGINA CŒLI.

SAID FOR THE ANGELUS IN PASCHAL TIME.

Joy to thee, O Queen of Heaven! alleluia. He whom thou wast meet to bear: alleluia. As He promised hath arisen: alleluia. Pour for us to Him thy prayer: alleluia.

V. Rejoice and be glad, O Virgin Mary: alleluia.

R. For the Lord hath risen indeed: alleluia.

Let us pray.

O God, who didst vouchsafe to give joy to the world through the Resurrection of Thy Son, our Lord Jesus Christ; grant, we beseech Thee, that, through His Mother, the Virgin Mary, we may obtain the joys of everlasting life. Through the same Christ our Lord. Amen.

GLORIA PATRI.

Glory be to the Father, and to the Son, and to the Holy Ghost. As it was in the beginning, is now, and ever shall be, world without end. Amen.

100 days for saying three Glorys, morning, noon, and evening, in thanksgiving for the graces given to our Blessed Lady, especially in her glorious Assumption.

DE PROFUNDIS.

Psalmus 129.

De profundis clamavi ad te, Domine: Domine, exaudi vocem meam.

Fiant aures tuæ intendentes in vocem deprecationis meæ.

Si iniquitates observaveris, Domine: Domine, quis sustinebit?

Quia apud te propitiatio est; et propter legem tuam sustinui te, Domine.

Sustinuit anima mea in verbo ejus: speravit anima mea in Domino.

A custodia matutina usque ad noctem: speret Israel in Domino.

Quia apud Dominum misericordia: et copiosa apud eum redemptio.

Et ipse redimet Israel ex omnibus iniquitatibus ejus.

V. Requiem æternam dona eis, Domine.

Et lux perpetua luceat eis.

V. Requiescant in pace.

R. Amen.

V. Domine, exaudi orationem meam.

R. Et clamor meus ad te veniat.

DE PROFUNDIS.

Out of the depths I have cried to Thee, O Lord: Lord, hear my voice.

Let Thine ears be attentive to the voice of my supplication.

If Thou, O Lord, wilt mark iniquities; Lord, who shall abide it?

Because with Thee there is merciful forgiveness; and by reason of Thy law I have waited for Thee, O Lord.

My soul hath relied on His word: my soul hath hoped in the Lord.

From the morning watch even until night, let Israel hope in the Lord.

Because with the Lord there is mercy, and with Him plentiful Redemption.

And He shall redeem Israel from all her iniquities.

V. Eternal rest give to them, O Lord.

R. And let perpetual light shine upon them.

May they rest in peace. Amen.

100 *days for saying the De Profundis or one Our Father, Hail Mary, and Eternal Rest, kneeling, at the sound of the bell, at nightfall.*

It may end thus—

V. Lord, hear my prayer.

R. And let my cry come unto Thee.

Oremus.

Fidelium Deus omnium conditor et redemptor, animabus famulorum famularumque tuarum remissionem cunctorum tribue peccatorum : ut indulgentiam quam semper optaverunt, piis supplicationibus consequantur; qui vivis et regnas cum Deo Patre in unitate Spiritus Sancti Deus, per omnia sæcula sæculorum. Amen.

Requiem æternam, &c.

SALVE REGINA.

Salve Regina, Mater misericordiæ, vita, dulcedo et spes nostra, salve. Ad te clamamus, exules filii Hevæ. Ad te suspiramus, gementes et flentes in hac lacrymarum valle. Eia ergo, Advocata nostra, illos tuos misericordes oculos ad nos converte, et Jesum benedictum fructum ventris tui, nobis post hoc exilium ostende, O clemens, o pia, o dulcis Virgo Maria.

MEMORARE.

Memorare, O piissima Virgo Maria, non esse auditum a sæculo quemquam ad tua currentem præsidia, tua implorantem auxilia, tua petentem suffragia, esse derelictum. Ego, tali animatus confidentia, ad te, Virgo virginum, Mater, curro. Ad te venio; coram te gemens peccator assisto. Noli, Mater Verbi, verba mea despicere, sed audi propitia et exaudi. Amen.

[300 *dies.*

Let us pray.

O God, the Creator and Redeemer of all the faithful, grant to the souls of Thy servants departed the remission of all their sins, that through pious supplications they may obtain that pardon which they have always desired; who livest and reignest with God the Father in the unity of the Holy Ghost, God, world without end. Amen.

Eternal rest, &c.

SALVE REGINA.

Hail, Holy Queen, Mother of Mercy, our life, our sweetness, and our hope. To thee do we cry, poor banished sons of Eve. To thee do we send our sighs, mourning and weeping in this vale of tears. Turn, then, most gracious Advocate, those thine eyes of mercy towards us; and after this our exile ended, show unto us the blessed fruit of thy womb, Jesus, O most clement, most pious, most sweet Virgin Mary.

MEMORARE.

Remember, O most gracious Virgin Mary, that never was it known that any one who fled to thy protection, implored thy help, and sought thy intercession, was left unaided. Inspired with this confidence, I fly unto thee, O Virgin of virgins, my Mother. To thee I come; before thee I stand, sinful and sorrowful. O Mother of the Word Incarnate, despise not my petitions, but in thy mercy hear and answer me. Amen.

[300 *days.*

DIVINE PRAISES.

To be said in reparation for Blasphemy.

Blessed be God.
Blessed be His Holy Name.
Blessed be Jesus Christ, true God and true Man.
Blessed be the Name of Jesus.
Blessed be Jesus in the Most Holy Sacrament of the Altar.
Blessed be the great Mother of God, Mary Most Holy.
Blessed be her holy and Immaculate Conception.
Blessed be the Name of Mary, Virgin and Mother.
Blessed be God in His Angels and in His Saints. [*One year.*

DAILY EXERCISES.

Morning Prayers.—Never omit to say at least a few prayers every morning. Morning prayer is the food of the soul on which its strength for the day depends.

Holy Mass.—"To begin well and to end better, two things," St. Philip Neri said, "are needed—to be devout to the most holy Mother of God and to hear Mass daily when there is no lawful hindrance."

Daily Duties.—*Fac quod facis,* "Do what Thou doest"—that is, do each duty at its proper time, as if it were the only one you had to do, and the last—*quasi unum et quasi ultimum.*

In beginning any work, sign yourself and say, "Oh, my God, I offer Thee this work."

Before Meals, sign yourself and say, *Benedictus benedicat*—"May the Blessed bless it."

After Meals, say, *Benedictus benedicatur*—" May the Blessed be blessed."

For a longer Grace see page 12.

Use the following ejaculations as occasion requires :—

In temptation—Lord save me, or I perish; Isai. xxxviii. 14; Jesu, Mary, Joseph.

At going forth—Incline unto my aid, O God: O Lord, make haste to help me; Ps. lxxx. 2.

On custody of sight—Turn away mine eyes, lest they behold vanity; Ps. cxviii. 7.

In conversation—Set, O Lord, a guard to my mouth, and a watch about my lips; Ps. cxl. 3.

After falling into any light fault—Humbly renew your purpose and begin again. Depression after a fault comes from wounded pride, and is often more sinful than the fault itself.

After a graver sin—Make an Act of Contrition, and go to confession *as soon as possible*.

To prevent relapses—Avoid the dangerous occasion. *Fuge cito, fuge procul, fuge semper; hoc fac et vives*—" Fly quickly, fly far, fly always. Do this, and thou shalt live."—ST. PHILIP NERI.

MORNING PRAYERS.

In the name of the Father, ✠ and of the Son, and of the Holy Ghost. Amen.

[50 *days.*

O God, the Creator and Ruler of all things, in whom we live and move and have our being, without whom we can do nothing; I give Thee thanks for Thy care of me in the night past, and for all Thy many blessings. I intend this day to do everything for Thy glory, in union with the intentions of Jesus and Mary on earth.

ACT OF FAITH.

O my God, I firmly believe in Thee, and in all that Thou hast revealed to Thy Holy Catholic Church, because Thou art Truth itself.

In this faith, and for this faith, I desire to live and to die.

ACT OF HOPE.

O my God, I hope in Thy infinite mercy, and through the merits of Jesus Christ, for pardon of all my sins, for grace to serve Thee, and for life everlasting.

In Thee, O Lord, have I hoped; let me not be confounded for ever.

ACT OF CHARITY.

O my God, I love Thee with my whole heart, and above all things, because Thou art Infinite Goodness, and for Thy sake I love my neighbour as myself.

Make me to love Thee ever more and more.

ACT OF CONTRITION.

O my God, I am heartily sorry for having offended Thee, and I detest my sins for love of Thee. I firmly resolve, by Thy grace, to sin no more. A contrite and humble heart, O God, Thou wilt not despise.

PATER. AVE. CREDO.

AN OBLATION.

O my Lady, Holy Mary, Queen of Perseverance, to thee, and to thy blessed charge and special keeping, and into the bosom of thy mercy, for this day and every day, and for the hour of my death, I commend myself, body and soul: my every hope and every joy, my every trouble and every sorrow, my life and my life's end, I commit to thee, that, by virtue of thy most holy intercession, and by thy merits, all that I have may be ordered, all that I do disposed, according to thy will, and that of thy Son. Amen.

Holy Michael the Archangel, defend us from our enemies.

St. Joseph, St. Philip, our Patron Saints, and all the Saints of God, intercede for us.

Angel of God, who art my guardian, to whose care I have been committed by the Divine Goodness, enlighten, guard, direct, and govern me this day.

May our Lord bless us, and preserve us from all evil, and bring us to life everlasting; and may the souls of the faithful through the mercy of God rest in peace. Amen.

An intention should be made every morning of gaining all the indulgences possible, and of applying them in general to the holy souls in Purgatory, or according to individual devotion.

Here may be said the Litany of the Holy Name.

LITANY OF THE MOST HOLY NAME OF JESUS.

An Indulgence of three hundred days was granted by Rescript, dated April 28, 1864, to the Faithful in England for the devout recitation of the Litany of the Most Holy Name, by our Most Holy Father Pope Pius IX., who at the same time prohibited any form but that of which the following is a translation, authorized by the Bishops.

Lord, have mercy on us.
Christ, have mercy on us.
Lord, have mercy on us.
Jesus, hear us.
Jesus, graciously hear us.
God the Father of heaven,
God the Son, Redeemer of the world,
God the Holy Ghost,
Holy Trinity, one God,
Jesus, Son of the living God,
Jesus, splendour of the Father,
Jesus, brightness of eternal light,
Jesus, King of Glory,
Jesus, Sun of Justice,
Jesus, Son of the Virgin Mary,
Jesus, most amiable,

Have mercy on us.

Jesus, most admirable,
Jesus, mighty God,
Jesus, Father of the world to come,
Jesus, Angel of great counsel,
Jesus, most powerful,
Jesus, most patient,
Jesus, most obedient,
Jesus, meek and humble of heart,
Jesus, lover of chastity,
Jesus, lover of us,
Jesus, God of peace,
Jesus, Author of life,
Jesus, example of virtues,
Jesus, zealous lover of souls,
Jesus, our God,
Jesus, our refuge,
Jesus, Father of the poor,
Jesus, treasure of the faithful,
Jesus, Good Shepherd,
Jesus, true light,
Jesus, eternal wisdom,
Jesus, infinite goodness,
Jesus, our way and our life,
Jesus, joy of Angels,
Jesus, King of Patriarchs,
Jesus, Master of Apostles,
Jesus, Teacher of Evangelists,

Have mercy on us.

Jesus, strength of Martyrs,
Jesus, light of Confessors,
Jesus, purity of Virgins,
Jesus, Crown of all Saints,   *} Have mercy on us.*

Be merciful unto us,
Spare us, O Jesus.
Be merciful unto us,
Graciously hear us, O Jesus.

From all evil,
From all sin,
From Thy wrath,
From the snares of the devil,
From the spirit of uncleanness,
From everlasting death,
From the neglect of thy Inspirations,
Through the mystery of thy holy Incar‑
   nation,
Through thy Nativity,
Through thine Infancy,
Through thy most divine life,
Through thy labours,
Through thine agony and passion,
Through thy Cross and dereliction,
Through thy faintness and weariness,
Through thy death and burial,
Through thy resurrection,
Through thine ascension,   *} Jesus, deliver us.*

Through thy joys,
Through thy glory, } *Jesus, deliver us.*

Lamb of God, who takest away the sins of the world,

Spare us, O Jesus.

Lamb of God, who takest away the sins of the world,

Graciously hear us, O Jesus.

Lamb of God, who takest away the sins of the world,

Have mercy on us, O Jesus.

Jesus hear us.

Jesus graciously hear us.

Let us pray.

O Lord Jesus Christ, who hast said: Ask, and ye shall receive; seek, and ye shall find; knock, and it shall be opened unto you; give, we beseech thee, to us who ask the grace of thy most divine love, that with all our heart, words, and works, we may love thee, and never cease to praise thee.

Make us, O Lord, to have a perpetual fear and love of thy holy Name, for thou never failest to govern those whom thou dost solidly establish in thy love. Through Jesus Christ our Lord. Amen.

EVENING PRAYERS.

In the name of the Father, ✠ and of the Son, and of the Holy Ghost. Amen.

I adore Thee, O my God; I believe in thee, I hope in Thee, and I love thee with my whole heart. I thank Thee for having created me, given me the true faith, and for all thy gifts of this day. Grant me the grace to know my sins and to be truly sorry for them.

Examine what sins you have committed this day, thinking where and with whom you have been; and afterwards say—

O my God, I am sorry from my heart for all my sins against Thee, because I have lost Heaven and deserved hell; and still more because I have offended Thee, who art so good and so merciful. I resolve, with Thy help, never more to sin, and always to fly from every occasion of sin.

Eternal Father, I offer Thee the most Precious Blood of Jesus Christ, in satisfaction for my sins, and for the wants of Holy Church. [100 *days.*

Our Father. Hail Mary. I Believe.

Sweet heart of Mary, be my salvation.
[300 *days.*

O my good Angel, watch over me.

May the Blessed Virgin, St. Joseph, St. Philip, and all the Saints, pray for us to our Lord, that we may be preserved this night from sin and all evils.

Jesus, Mary, Joseph, I give you my heart and my soul.

Jesus, Mary, Joseph, assist me in my last agony.

Jesus, Mary, Joseph, may I expire in peace with you. [300 *days*.

May the souls of the faithful, through the mercy of God, rest in peace. Amen.

Here may be said the Litany of the Blessed Virgin (Latin, see page 101) *or the* "*Nunc Dimittis.*"

LITANY OF THE BLESSED VIRGIN.

300 *days*.

Lord, have mercy on us.
Lord, have mercy on us.
Christ, have mercy on us.
Christ, have mercy on us.
Lord, have mercy on us.
Lord, have mercy on us.
Christ, hear us.

Christ, graciously hear us.

God the Father of Heaven,
God the Son, Redeemer of the world,
God the Holy Ghost,
Holy Trinity one God,
} *Have mercy on us.*

Holy Mary, *Pray for us.*
Holy Mother of God,
Holy Virgin of Virgins,
Mother of Christ,
Mother of divine grace,
Mother most pure,
Mother most chaste,
Mother inviolate,
Mother undefiled,
Mother most amiable,
Mother most admirable,
Mother of our Creator,
Mother of our Saviour,
Virgin most prudent,
Virgin most venerable,
Virgin most renowned,
Virgin most powerful,
Virgin most merciful,
Virgin most faithful,
Mirror of justice,
Seat of Wisdom,
} *Pray for us.*

Litany.

Cause of our joy,
Spiritual Vessel,
Vessel of honour,
Vessel of singular devotion,
Mystical Rose,
Tower of David,
Tower of ivory,
House of gold,
Ark of the covenant,
Gate of heaven,
Morning star,
Health of the sick,
Refuge of sinners,
Comforter of the afflicted,
Help of Christians,
Queen of Angels,
Queen of Patriarchs,
Queen of Prophets,
Queen of Apostles,
Queen of Martyrs,
Queen of Confessors,
Queen of Virgins,
Queen of all Saints,
Queen conceived without original sin,

} *Pray for us.*

Lamb of God, who takest away the sins of the world,
Spare us, O Lord.

Lamb of God, who takest away the sins of the world,

Graciously hear us, O Lord.

Lamb of God who takest away the sins of the world,

Have mercy on us.

Ant. We fly to thy patronage, O Holy Mother of God, despise not our petitions in our necessities; but deliver us always from all dangers, O glorious and Blessed Virgin.

V. Pray for us, O Holy Mother of God.

R. That we may be made worthy of the promises of Christ.

Let us pray.

Defend, O Lord, we beseech Thee, by the intercession of the Blessed Mary ever Virgin, this Thy family from all adversity; and mercifully protect us, who prostrate ourselves before Thee with our whole hearts, from the snares of our enemies. Through Christ our Lord. Amen.

CANTICUM SIMEONIS.

Nunc dimittis servum tuum, domine, secundum verbum tuum in pace.

Quia viderunt oculi mei salutare tuum.

Quod parasti ante faciem omnium populorum.

Lumen ad revelationem gentium et gloriam plebis tuæ Israel.

Gloria Patri, &c.

Ant. Salva nos, Domine, vigilantes, custodi nos dormientes, ut vigilemus cum Christo et requiescamus in pace (tempore Paschali Alleluia).

THE CANTICLE OF SIMEON.

Now dost thou dismiss thy servant, O Lord, in peace: according to Thy word.

For mine eyes have seen Thy salvation.

Which Thou hast prepared before the face of all Thy people.

A light to enlighten the Gentiles, and the glory of Thy people Israel.

Glory be to the Father, &c.

Ant. Save us, O Lord, when we are awake, and keep us while we sleep, that we may watch with Christ, and rest in peace (In Paschal time, Alleluia).

AD ASPERSIONEM AQUÆ BENEDICTÆ.

Ant. Asperges me, Domine, hyssopo, et mundabor: lavabis me, et super nivem dealbabor. *Ps.* Miserere mei, Deus, secundum magnam misericordiam tuam. *V.* Gloria Patri, &c.

Ant. Asperges me.

V. Ostende nobis, Domine, misericordiam tuam.
R. Et salutare tuum da nobis.
V. Domine, exaudi orationem meam.
R. Et clamor meus ad te veniat.
V. Dominus vobiscum.
R. Et cum spiritu tuo.

Oremus.

Exaudi nos, Domine sancte, Pater omnipotens, æterne Deus; et mittere digneris sanctum Angelum tuum de cœlis, qui custodiat, foveat, protegat, visitet, atque defendat omnes habitantes in hoc habitaculo. Per Christum Dominum nostrum. Amen.

Ant. Vidi aquam egredientem de templo a latere dextro, Alleluia; et omnes ad quos pervenit aqua ista salvi facti sunt, et dicent, Alleluia. *Ps.* Confitemini Domino, quoniam bonus; quoniam in sæculum misericordia ejus. Gloria, &c.

Before Mass.

THE ASPERGES.

Ant. Thou shalt sprinkle me with hyssop, O Lord, and I shall be cleansed: Thou shalt wash me, and I shall be made whiter than snow. *Ps.* Have mercy on me, O God, according to Thy great mercy. *V.* Glory be, &c.

Ant. Thou shalt sprinkle me.

The Priest, having returned to the foot of the Altar, says:—

V. Show us, O Lord, Thy mercy.
R. And grant us Thy salvation.
V. O Lord, hear my prayer.
R. And let my cry come unto Thee.
V. The Lord be with you.
R. And with thy spirit.

Let us pray.

Hear us, O holy Lord, Almighty Father, Eternal God; and vouchsafe to send Thy holy Angel from heaven, to guard, cherish, protect, visit, and defend all that are assembled in this house. Through Christ our Lord. Amen.

From Easter to Whit Sunday, inclusively, instead of the foregoing Antiphon, the following is sung, and Alleluia is added to the *V.* (*Ostende nobis*), and also to the *R.* (*Et salutare*).

Ant. I saw water flowing from the right side of the temple, Alleluia; and all to whom that water came were saved, and they shall say, Alleluia. *Ps.* Praise the Lord, for He is good; for His mercy endureth for ever. Glory, &c.

ORDO MISSÆ.

Sacerdos ante infimum gradum Altaris incipit missam.

In Nomine Patris, ✠ et Filii, et Spiritus Sancti. Amen.
Introibo ad altare Dei.
R. Ad Deum, qui lætificat juventutem meam.

Psalmus xlii.

S. Judica me, Deus, et discerne causam meam de gente non sancta; ab homine iniquo et doloso erue me.
M. Quia tu es, Deus, fortitudo mea, quare me repulisti? et quare tristis incedo dum affligit me inimicus?
S. Emitte lucem tuam et veritatem tuam: ipsa me deduxerunt et adduxerunt in montem sanctum tuum, et in tabernacula tua.
M. Et introibo ad altare Dei: ad Deum, qui lætificat juventutem meam.
S. Confitebor tibi in cithara, Deus, Deus meus: quare tristis es, anima mea? et quare conturbas me?
M. Spera in Deo, quoniam adhuc confitebor illi: salutare vultus mei, et Deus meus.
S. Gloria Patri, et Filio, et Spiritui Sancto.
M. Sicut erat in principio, et nunc, et semper, et in sæcula sæculorum. Amen.
V. Introibo ad altare Dei.
R. Ad Deum, qui lætificat juventutem meam.
V. Adjutorium nostrum in nomine Domini.
R. Qui fecit cœlum et terram.

ORDINARY OF THE MASS.

The Priest begins at the foot of the Altar.

In the name of the Father, ✠ and of the Son, and of the Holy Ghost. Amen.

I will go unto the altar of God.

R. To God, who giveth joy to my youth.

Psalm xlii.

P. Judge me, O God, and distinguish my cause from the nation that is not holy; deliver me from the unjust and deceitful man.

R. For Thou, O God, art my strength, why hast Thou cast me off? and why do I go sorrowful whilst the enemy afflicteth me?

P. Send forth Thy light and Thy truth; they have conducted me and brought me unto Thy holy mount, and into Thy tabernacles.

R. And I will go unto the altar of God: to God, who giveth joy to my youth.

P. I will praise Thee on the harp, O God, my God: why art Thou sorrowful, O my soul? and why dost Thou disquiet me?

R. Hope in God, for I will still give praise to Him: who is the salvation of my countenance, and my God.

P. Glory be to the Father, and to the Son, and to the Holy Ghost.

R. As it was in the beginning, is now, and ever shall be, world without end. Amen.

V. I will go unto the altar of God.

R. To God, who giveth joy to my youth.

V. Our help is in the name of the Lord.

R. Who hath made heaven and earth.

Ordo Missæ.

Deinde junctis manibus, profunde inclinatus, facit Confessionem.

S. Confiteor Deo, &c. (page 13).
M. Misereatur tui, &c.
M. Confiteor Deo, &c.

Postea Sacerdos junctis manibus facit absolutionem, dicens—

S. Misereatur vestri, &c.

Signat se signo Crucis, dicens—

S. ✠ Indulgentiam, &c.

Et inclinatus, prosequitur:

V. Deus, tu conversus vivificabis nos.
R. Et plebs tua lætabitur in te.
V. Ostende nobis, Domine, misericordiam tuam.
R. Et salutare tuum da nobis.
V. Domine, exaudi orationem meam.
R. Et clamor meus ad te veniat.
V. Dominus vobiscum.
R. Et cum spiritu tuo.

Ascendens ad Altare, dicit secreto—

Aufer a nobis, quæsumus, Domine, iniquitates nostras; ut ad Sancta sanctorum puris mereamur mentibus introire. Per Christum Dominum nostrum. Amen.

Deinde, super Altare inclinatus, dicit—

Oramus te, Domine, per merita Sanctorum tuorum, quorum reliquiæ hic sunt, et omnium Sanctorum, ut indulgere digneris omnia peccata mea. Amen.

Ordinary of the Mass. 45

Then joining his hands and humbly bowing down, he says the Confession:

P. I confess, &c.
R. May Almighty God, &c.
R. I confess, &c.

Then the Priest, with his hands joined, gives the Absolution, saying—

P. May Almighty God, &c.

Signing himself with the sign of the Cross, he says—

P. ✠ May the Almighty, &c.

Then, bowing down, he proceeds:

V. Thou wilt turn again, O God, and quicken us.
R. And Thy people shall rejoice in Thee.
V. Show us, O Lord Thy mercy.
R. And grant us Thy salvation.
V. O Lord, hear my prayer.
R. And let my cry come unto Thee.
V. The Lord be with you.
R. And with thy spirit.

Going up to the Altar, he says secretly—

Take away from us our iniquities, we beseech Thee, O Lord; that we may be worthy to enter with pure minds into the Holy of Holies. Through Christ Jesus our Lord. Amen.

Bowing down over the Altar, he says—

We beseech Thee, O Lord, by the merits of Thy Saints, whose relics are here, and of all the Saints, that Thou wouldst vouchsafe to forgive me all my sins. Amen.

Ordo Missæ.

[In Missa solemni Celebrans benedicit incensum.]
Deinde, signans se signo Crucis, incipit Introitum.

Kyrie eleison (*ter*).
Christe eleison (*ter*).
Kyrie eleison (*ter*).

Postea in medio Altaris, extendens et jungens manus caputque aliquantulum inclinans, dicit—

Gloria in excelsis Deo; et in terra pax hominibus bonæ voluntatis. Laudamus Te; benedicimus Te; adoramus Te; glorificamus Te. Gratias agimus Tibi propter magnam gloriam tuam, Domine Deus, Rex cœlestis, Deus Pater omnipotens. Domine Fili unigenite Jesu Christe; Domine Deus, Agnus Dei, Filius Patris, qui tollis peccata mundi, miserere nobis; qui tollis peccata mundi, suscipe deprecationem nostram: qui sedes ad dexteram Patris, miserere nobis. Quoniam Tu solus sanctus: Tu solus Dominus: Tu solus altissimus, Jesu Christe, cum Sancto Spiritu, in gloria Dei Patris. Amen.

Deinde osculatur Altare, et, versus ad populum, dicit—

℣. Dominus vobiscum.
℟. Et cum spiritu tuo.

---

* The Introit, the Collects, Epistle, Gradual, Gospel, Offertory, Secrets, Communion and Post-Communions, are variable, and may be found in the Missal.

Ordinary of the Mass. 47

[At High Mass the Altar is here incensed.] Then the Priest, signing himself with the sign of the Cross, reads the Introit.*

The Kyrie Eleison is then said:

Lord, have mercy upon us (*three times*).
Christ, have mercy upon us (*three times*).
Lord, have mercy upon us (*three times*).

Afterwards, standing at the middle of the Altar, extending, and then joining his hands, he says the Gloria in Excelsis.†

Glory be to God on high, and on earth peace to men of good will. We praise Thee; we bless Thee; we adore Thee; we glorify Thee. We give Thee thanks for Thy great glory, O Lord God, heavenly King. God the Father Almighty. O Lord Jesus Christ, the only-begotten Son: O Lord God, Lamb of God, Son of the Father, who takest away the sins of the world, have mercy on us: Thou who takest away the sins of the world, receive our prayers: Thou who sittest at the right hand of the Father, have mercy on us. For thou only art holy: Thou only art the Lord: Thou only, O Jesus Christ, with the Holy Ghost, art most high in the Glory of God the Father. Amen.

The Priest kisses the Altar, and, turning to the people, says—

V. The Lord be with you.
R. And with thy spirit.

---

† The *Gloria* is omitted on Sundays during Advent, and from Septuagesima to Easter, also in ferial Masses, and Masses for the Dead.

Tunc sequuntur orationes et Epistola; hac finita, dicitur—

℟. Deo gratias.

Deinde Graduale, Tractus, Alleluia, aut Sequentia.
Ante Evangelium.

Munda cor meum ac labia mea, omnipotens Deus, qui labia Isaiæ prophetæ calculo mundasti ignito: ita me tua grata miseratione dignare mundare, ut sanctum Evangelium tuum digne valeam nuntiare. Per Christum Dominum nostrum. Amen.

Dominus sit in corde meo et in labiis meis, ut digne et competenter annuntiem Evangelium suum. Amen.

℣. Dominus vobiscum.

℟. Et cum spiritu tuo.

℣. Sequentia (*vel* Initium) sancti Evangelii secundum *N*.

℟. Gloria tibi, Domine.

Tunc legitur Evangelium; hoc finito, dicitur—

℟. Laus tibi, Christe.

Per Evangelica dicta deleantur nostra delicta.

SYMBOLUM NICAENUM.

Credo in unum Deum, Patrem omnipotentem, Factorem cœli et terræ, visibilium omnium et invisibilium.

Et in unum Dominum Jesum Christum, Filium Dei unigenitum, et ex Patre natum ante omnia sæcula. Deum de Deo; Lumen de lumine; Deum verum de Deo vero; genitum

Ordinary of the Mass.

Then follow the Collects and the Epistle, after which is said—

R. Thanks be to God.

Then the Gradual, Tract, Alleluia, or Sequence.

Before the Gospel.

Cleanse my heart and my lips, O Almighty God, who didst cleanse the lips of the prophet Isaias with a burning coal: and vouchsafe, through Thy gracious mercy, so to purify me, that I may worthily proclaim Thy holy Gospel. Through Christ our Lord. Amen.

The Lord be in my heart and on my lips, that I may worthily, and in a becoming manner, announce His holy Gospel. Amen.

V. The Lord be with you.

R. And with thy spirit.

V. The continuation (*or* beginning) of the holy Gospel according to *N.*

R. Glory be to Thee, O Lord.

Then is read the Gospel, after which is said—

R. Praise be to Thee, O Christ.

By the words of the Gospel may our sins be blotted out.

NICENE CREED.

I believe in one God, the Father Almighty, Maker of heaven and earth, and of all things visible and invisible.

And in one Lord Jesus Christ, the only begotten Son of God, born of the Father before all ages. God of God; Light of light; true God of true God; begotten, not made; consubstan-

non factum ; consubstantialem Patri, per quem omnia facta sunt. Qui propter nos homines, et propter nostram salutem, descendit de cœlis, et incarnatus est de Spiritu Sancto, ex Maria Virgine : ET HOMO FACTUS EST. [*Hic genuflectitur.*] Crucifixus etiam pro nobis : sub Pontio Pilato passus et sepultus est. Et resurrexit tertia die secundum Scripturas ; et ascendit in cœlum, sedet ad dexteram Patris : et iterum venturus est cum gloria judicare vivos et mortuos : cujus regni non erit finis.

Et in Spiritum Sanctum, Dominum et vivificantem, qui ex Patre Filioque procedit : qui cum Patre et Filio simul adoratur et conglorificatur : qui locutus est per prophetas. Et unam sanctam Catholicam et Apostolicam Ecclesiam. Confiteor unum baptisma in remissionem peccatorum. Et expecto resurrectionem mortuorum, et vitam venturi sæculi. Amen.

V. Dominus vobiscum.

R. Et cum spiritu tuo.

Postea legit Offertorium, et accipiens patenam cum hostia, dicit—

Suscipe, sancte Pater, omnipotens, æterne Deus, hanc immaculatam Hostiam, quam ego indignus famulus tuus offero tibi, Deo meo vivo et vero, pro innumerabilibus peccatis, et offensionibus, et negligentiis meis, et pro omnibus circumstantibus, sed et pro omnibus fidelibus Christianis, vivis atque defunctis ; ut mihi et illis proficiat ad salutem in vitam æternam. Amen.

Ordinary of the Mass. 51

tial with the Father, by whom all things were made. Who for us men, and for our salvation, came down from heaven, and was incarnate by the Holy Ghost of the Virgin Mary: AND WAS MADE MAN. [*Here the people kneel down.*] He was crucified also for us, suffered under Pontius Pilate, and was buried. The third day He rose again according to the Scriptures, and ascended into heaven, and sitteth at the right hand of the Father: and He shall come again with glory to judge both the living and the dead: of whose kingdom there shall be no end.

And I believe in the Holy Ghost, the Lord and Life-giver, who proceedeth from the Father and the Son: who together with the Father and the Son is adored and glorified: who spake by the prophets. And one holy Catholic and Apostolic Church. I confess one baptism for the remission of sins. And I look for the resurrection of the dead, and the life of the world to come. Amen.

V. The Lord be with you.
R. And with thy spirit.

Then he reads the Offertory, and taking the Paten with the Host, says—

Accept, O holy Father, Almighty, Eternal God, this immaculate Host, which I, Thy unworthy servant, offer unto Thee, my living and true God, for my innumerable sins, offences, and negligences, and for all here present; as also for all faithful Christians, both living and dead, that it may be profitable for my own and for their salvation unto life eternal. Amen.

Infundens vinum et aquam in Calicem, dicit—

Deus, ✠ qui humanæ substantiæ dignitatem mirabiliter condidisti, et mirabilius reformasti; da nobis per hujus aquæ et vini mysterium, ejus divinitatis esse consortes, qui humanitatis nostræ fieri dignatus est particeps, Jesus Christus, Filius tuus, Dominus noster: qui tecum vivat et regnat in unitate Spiritus Sancti Deus, per omnia sæcula sæculorum. Amen.

Accipit Calicem et offert, dicens—

Offerimus tibi, Domine, calicem salutaris, tuam deprecantes clementiam, ut in conspectu divinæ Majestatis tuæ, pro nostra et totius mundi salute cum odore suavitatis ascendat. Amen.

Et inclinatus, dicit—

In spiritu humilitatis, et in animo contrito, suscipiamur a te, Domine; et sic fiat sacrificium nostrum in conspectu tuo hodie, ut placeat tibi, Domine Deus.

Elevat oculos et expandens manus, dicit—

Veni, sanctificator, omnipotens æterne Deus, et bene ✠ dic hoc sacrificium, tuo sancto nomini præparatum.

Si solemniter celebrat, benedicit incensum, dicens—

Per intercessionem beati Michaelis Archangeli, stantis a dextris altaris incensi, et omnium electorum suorum, incensum istud dignetur Dominus bene ✠ dicere, et in odorem, suavitatis accipere. Per Christum Dominum nostrum. Amen.

Ordinary of the Mass. 53

Pouring wine and water into the Chalice, he says—

O God, ✠ who, in creating human nature, didst wonderfully dignify it, and hast still more wonderfully renewed it; grant that, by the mystery of this water and wine, we may be made partakers of His divinity who vouchsafed to become partaker of our humanity, Jesus Christ, Thy Son, our Lord; who liveth and reigneth with Thee in the unity of, &c.

Offering up the Chalice, he says—

We offer unto Thee, O Lord, the chalice of salvation, beseeching Thy clemency, that, in the sight of Thy Divine Majesty, it may ascend with the odour of sweetness, for our salvation, and for that of the whole world. Amen.

Bowing down, he says—

In the spirit of humility, and with a contrite heart, let us be received by Thee, O Lord; and grant that the sacrifice we offer in Thy sight this day may be pleasing to Thee, O Lord God.

Elevating his eyes and stretching out his hands, he says—

Come, O sanctifier, Almighty, Eternal God, and bless ✠ this sacrifice, prepared to Thy holy Name.

At High Mass he blesses the Incense, saying—

May the Lord, by the intercession of blessed Michael the Archangel, standing at the right hand of the altar of incense, and of all His elect, vouchsafe to bless ✠ this incense, and receive it as an odour of sweetness. Through, &c. Amen.

Ordo Missæ.

Incensat oblata, dicens—

Incensum istud a te benedictum ascendat ad te, Domine, et descendat super nos misericordia tua.

Deinde incensat Altare, dicens—

Dirigatur, Domine, oratio mea sicut incensum in conspectu tuo : elevatio manuum mearum sacrificium vespertinum. Pone, Domine, custodiam ori meo, et ostium circumstantiæ labiis meis, ut non declinet cor meum in verba malitiæ, ad excusandas excusationes in peccatis.

Dum reddit thuribulum Diacono, dicit—

Accendat in nobis Dominus ignem sui amoris, et flammam æternæ caritatis. Amen.

Sacerdos lavat manus, dicens :—

Lavabo inter innocentes manus meas : et circumdabo altare tuum, Domine. Ut audiam vocem laudis : et enarrem universa mirabilia tua. Domine, dilexi decorem domus tuæ et locum habitationis gloriæ tuæ. Ne perdas cum impiis, Deus, animam meam : et cum viris sanguinum vitam meam. In quorum manibus iniquitates sunt : dextera eorum repleta est muneribus. Ego autem in innocentia mea ingressus sum : redime me, et miserere mei. Pes meus stetit in directo : in ecclesiis benedicam te, Domine. Gloria, &c.

Ordinary of the Mass. 55

He incenses the Bread and Wine, saying—

May this incense which Thou hast blessed, O Lord, ascend to thee, and may Thy mercy descend upon us.

Then he incenses the Altar, saying—

Let my prayer, O Lord, ascend like incense in Thy sight: and the lifting up of my hands be as an evening sacrifice. Set a watch, O Lord, before my mouth, and a door round about my lips, that my heart may not incline to evil words, to make excuses in sins.

Giving the thurible to the Deacon, he says—

May the Lord enkindle in us the fire of His love, and the flame of everlasting charity. Amen.

Washing his fingers, he recites the following:—

I will wash my hands among the innocent: and will encompass Thy altar, O Lord. That I may hear the voice of praise, and tell of all Thy marvellous works. I have loved, O Lord, the beauty of Thy house, and the place where Thy glory dwelleth. Take not away my soul, O God, with the wicked, nor my life with bloody men. In whose hands are iniquities: their right hand is filled with gifts. As for me, I have walked in my innocence: redeem me, and have mercy upon me. My foot hath stood in the right path: in the churches I will bless Thee, O Lord. Glory, &c.

Inclinatus in medio Altaris, dicit—

Suscipe, sancta Trinitas, hanc oblationem quam tibi offerimus ob memoriam Passionis, Resurrectionis, et Ascensionis Jesu Christi Domini nostri: et in honorem beatæ Mariæ semper Virginis, et beati Joannis Baptistæ, et sanctorum Apostolorum Petri et Pauli, et istorum et omnium Sanctorum : ut illis proficiat ad honorem, nobis autem ad salutem: et illi pro nobis intercedere dignentur in cœlis, quorum memoriam agimus in terris. Per eundem, &c.

Et versus ad populum, dicit—

Orate, fratres, ut meum ac vestrum sacrificium acceptabile fiat apud Deum Patrem omnipotentem.

R. Suscipiat Dominus sacrificium de manibus tuis, ad laudem et gloriam nominis sui, ad utilitatem quoque nostram, totiusque Ecclesiæ suæ sanctæ.

Orationes secretas subjungit. Postea, clara voce, dicit,—

V. Per omnia sæcula sæculorum.
R. Amen.
V. Dominus vobiscum.
R. Et cum spiritu tuo.
V. Sursum corda.
R. Habemus ad Dominum.
V. Gratias agamus Domino Deo nostro.
R. Dignum et justum est.

Ordinary of the Mass.

Bowing before the Altar, he says—

Receive, O Holy Trinity, this oblation, which we make to Thee, in memory of the Passion, Resurrection, and Ascension of our Lord Jesus Christ, and in honour of the Blessed Mary ever Virgin, of Blessed John Baptist, the holy Apostles Peter and Paul, of these and of all the Saints: that it may be available to their honour and our salvation: and may they vouchsafe to intercede for us in heaven, whose memory we celebrate on earth. Through, &c.

Turning to the people, he says—

Brethren, pray that my sacrifice and yours may be acceptable to God the Father Almighty.

R. May the Lord receive the sacrifice from thy hands, to the praise and glory of His Name, to our benefit, and to that of all His holy Church.

He then recites the Secret Prayers, and afterwards says in an audible voice—

V. World without end.
R. Amen.
V. The Lord be with you.
R. And with thy spirit.
V. Lift up your hearts.
R. We have them lifted up unto the Lord.
V. Let us give thanks to the Lord our God.
R. It is meet and just.

Vere dignum et justum est, æquum et salutare, nos tibi semper et ubique gratias agere, Domine sancte, Pater omnipotens, æterne Deus. Per Christum Dominum nostrum : per quem Majestatem tuam laudant angeli, adorant dominationes, tremunt potestates, cœli cœlorumque virtutes, ac beata seraphim, socia exultatione concelebrant. Cum quibus et nostras voces, ut admitti jubeas deprecamur, supplici confessione dicentes : Sanctus, sanctus, sanctus, Dominus Deus Sabaoth. Pleni sunt cœli et terra gloria tua. Hosanna in excelsis. Benedictus qui venit in nomine Domini. Hosanna in excelsis.

CANON MISSÆ.

Te igitur, clementissime Pater, per Jesum Christum Filium tuum Dominum nostrum, supplices rogamus ac petimus uti accepta habeas et benedicas hæc ✠ dona, hæc ✠ munera, hæc ✠ sancta sacrificia illibata, in primis quæ tibi offerimus pro Ecclesia tua sancta Catholica : quam pacificare, custodire, adunare, et regere digneris toto orbe terrarum, una cum famulo Papa nostro *N.*, et Antistite nostro *N.*, et omnibus orthodoxis, atque Catholicæ et Apostolicæ Fidei cultoribus.

COMMEMORATIO PRO VIVIS.

Memento, Domine, famulorum famularumque tuarum, *N.* et *N.*

It is truly meet and just, right and salutary, that we should always, and in all places, give thanks to Thee, O holy Lord, Father Almighty, Eternal God. Through Christ our Lord: through whom the Angels praise Thy Majesty, the dominations adore, the powers do hold in awe, the heavens, and the virtues of the heavens, and the blessed seraphim, do celebrate with united joy. In union with whom, we beseech Thee that Thou wouldst command our voices also to be admitted with suppliant confession, saying: Holy, holy, holy, Lord God of Sabaoth. Heaven and earth are full of Thy Glory. Hosanna in the highest. Blessed is He that cometh in the name of the Lord. Hosanna in the highest.

CANON OF THE MASS.

We therefore humbly pray and beseech Thee, most merciful Father, through Jesus Christ Thy Son, our Lord [*he kisses the Altar*], that Thou wouldst vouchsafe to accept and bless these ✠ gifts, these ✠ presents, these ✠ holy, unspotted sacrifices, which, in the first place, we offer Thee for Thy holy Catholic Church, to which vouchsafe to grant peace: as also to protect, unite, and govern it throughout the world, together with Thy servant *N.* our Pope, *N.* our Bishop, as also all orthodox believers and professors of the Catholic and Apostolic Faith.

COMMEMORATION OF THE LIVING.

Be mindful, O Lord, of Thy servants, *N.* and *N.*

Orat aliquantulum pro quibus orare intendit, deinde manibus extensis prosequitur:

Et omnium circumstantium, quorum tibi fides cognita est, et nota devotio: pro quibus tibi offerimus, vel qui tibi offerunt hoc sacrificium laudis, pro se, suisque omnibus, pro redemptione animarum suarum, pro spe salutis et incolumitatis suæ: tibique reddunt vota sua, æterno Deo, vivo et vero.

Communicantes, et memoriam venerantes, imprimis gloriosæ semper Virginis Mariæ, Genitricis Dei et Domini nostri Jesu Christi: sed et beatorum Apostolorum ac Martyrum tuorum, Petri et Pauli, Andreæ, Jacobi, Joannis, Thomæ, Jacobi, Philippi, Bartholomæi, Matthæi, Simonis et Thaddæi; Lini, Cleti, Clementis, Xysti, Cornelii, Cypriani, Laurentii, Chrysogoni, Joannis et Pauli, Cosmæ et Damiani, et omnium Sanctorum tuorum; quorum meritis precibusque concedas, ut in omnibus protectionis tuæ muniamur auxilio. Per eumdem Christum Dominum nostrum. Amen.

Tenens manus expansas super Oblata, dicit—

Hanc igitur oblationem servitutis nostræ, sed et cunctæ familiæ tuæ, quæsumus, Domine, ut placatus accipias; diesque nostros in tua pace disponas, atque ab æterna damnatione nos eripi, et in electorum tuorum jubeas grege numerari. Per Christum Dominum nostrum. Amen.

He pauses, and prays silently for those he intends to pray for, and proceeds:

And of all here present, whose faith and devotion are known unto Thee: for whom we offer, or who offer up to Thee, this sacrifice of praise for themselves, their families and friends, for the redemption of their souls, for the hope of their safety and salvation, and who pay their vows to Thee, the Eternal, Living, and True God.

Communicating with, and honouring in the first place the memory of the glorious and ever Virgin Mary, Mother of our Lord and God Jesus Christ; as also of the Blessed Apostles and Martyrs, Peter and Paul, Andrew, James, John, Thomas, James, Philip, Bartholomew, Matthew, Simon and Thaddeus, Linus, Cletus, Clement, Xystus, Cornelius, Cyprian, Lawrence, Chrysogonus, John and Paul, Cosmas and Damian, and of all Thy Saints; by whose merits and prayers grant that we may always be defended by the help of Thy protection. Through the same Christ our Lord. Amen.

Spreading his hands over the Oblation, he says—

We therefore beseech Thee, O Lord, graciously to accept this oblation of our service, as also of Thy whole family; dispose our days in Thy peace, command us to be delivered from eternal damnation, and to be numbered in the flock of Thy elect. Through Christ our Lord. Amen.

Quam oblationem, tu Deus, in omnibus, quæsumus, benedic ✠ tam, adscrip ✠ tam, ra ✠ tam, rationabilem, acceptabilemque facere digneris; ut nobis cor ✠ pus et san ✠ guis fiat dilectissimi Filii tui Domini nostri Jesu Christi.

Qui pridie quam pateretur [*accipit hostiam*], accepit panem in sanctas ac venerabiles manus suas [*elevat oculos ad cœlum*], et elevatis oculis in cœlum, ad te Deum Patrem suum omnipotentem, tibi gratias agens, benedixit, fregit, deditque discipulis suis, dicens: Accípite, et manducate ex hoc omnes; HOC EST ENIM CORPUS MEUM.

Prolatis verbis consecrationis, statim Hostiam consecratam genuflexus adorat; surgit, ostendit populo, reponit super Altare, iterum adorat.

Simili modo postquam cœnatum est, accipiens et hunc præclarum calicem in sanctas ac venerabiles manus suas, item tibi gratias agens, bene ✠ dixit, deditque discipulis suis, dicens: Accipite et bibite ex eo omnes; HIC EST ENIM CALIX SANGUINIS MEI NOVI ET ÆTERNI TESTAMENTI; MYSTERIUM FIDEI; QUI PRO VOBIS ET PRO MULTIS EFFUNDETUR IN REMISSIONEM PECCATORUM.

Hæc quotiescumque feceritis, in mei memoriam facietis.

Genuflexus, adorat, surgit, ostendi Calicem populo et iterum adorat.

Unde et memores, Domine, nos servi tui, sed

Which oblation do Thou, O God, vouchsafe in all things to make blessed, ✠ approved, ✠ ratified, ✠ reasonable, and acceptable, that it may become to us the body ✠ and ✠ blood of Thy most beloved Son Jesus Christ our Lord.

Who the day before He suffered took bread [*he takes the Host*] into His holy and venerable hands [*he raises his eyes to heaven*], and with His eyes lifted up towards heaven, to Thee, God, His Almighty Father, giving thanks to Thee, did bless, break, and give to His disciples, saying: Take, and eat ye all of this; FOR THIS IS MY BODY.

After pronouncing the words of consecration, the Priest, kneeling, adores the Sacred Host, and rising, he elevates It, and again adores It.

(At the Elevation, the bell is rung thrice.)

In like manner after He had supped [*he takes the chalice in both his hands*], taking also this excellent Chalice into His holy and venerable hands, and giving Thee thanks, He bless✠ed, and gave to His disciples, saying: Take, and drink ye all of this; FOR THIS IS THE CHALICE OF MY BLOOD OF THE NEW AND ETERNAL TESTAMENT; THE MYSTERY OF FAITH; WHICH SHALL BE SHED FOR YOU, AND FOR MANY, TO THE REMISSION OF SINS.

As often as ye do these things, ye shall do them in remembrance of Me.

Kneeling, he adores, and rising, elevates the Chalice, and again adores.

Wherefore, O Lord, we Thy servants, as also

et plebs tua sancta, ejusdem Christi Filii tui Domini nostri tam beatæ passionis, necnon et ab inferis resurrectionis, sed et in cœlos gloriosæ ascensionis : offerimus præclaræ Majestati tuæ, de tuis donis ac datis, Hostiam ✠ puram, Hostiam ✠ sanctam, Hostiam ✠ immaculatam, Panem ✠ sanctum vitæ æternæ, et Calicem ✠ salutis perpetuæ.

Extensis manibus, prosequitur—

Supra quæ propitio ac sereno vultu respicere digneris, et accepta habere, sicuti accepta habere dignatus es munera pueri tui justi Abel, et sacrificium Patriarchæ nostri Abrahæ; et quod tibi obtulit summus sacerdos tuus Melchisedech, sanctum sacrificium, immaculatam hostiam.

Profunde inclinatus, dicit—

Supplices te rogamus, omnipotens Deus, jube hæc perferri per manus sancti Angeli tui in sublime altare tuum, in conspectu divinæ Majestatis tuæ ut quotquot ex hac altaris participatione, sacrosanctum Filii tui Corpus ✠ et ✠ Sanguinem sumpserimus omni benedictione cœlesti et gratia repleamur. Per eumdem Christum Dominum nostrum. Amen.

COMMEMORATIO PRO DEFUNCTIS.

Memento etiam, Domine, famulorum famularumque tuarum *N.* et *N.*, qui nos præcesserunt cum signo fidei, et dormiunt in somno pacis.

Canon of the Mass. 65

Thy holy people, calling to mind the Blessed Passion of the same Christ Thy Son our Lord, His Resurrection from Hell, and glorious Ascension into heaven, offer unto Thy most excellent Majesty, of Thy gifts and grants, a pure ✠ Host, a holy ✠ Host, an immaculate ✠ Host, the holy ✠ Bread of eternal life, and the Chalice ✠ of everlasting salvation.

Extending his hands, he proceeds—

Upon which vouchsafe to look with a propitious and serene countenance, and to accept them, as Thou wert graciously pleased to accept the gifts of Thy just servant Abel, and the sacrifice of our Patriarch Abraham, and that which Thy high-priest Melchisedech offered to Thee, a holy sacrifice, an immaculate host.

Bowing down, he says—

We most humbly beseech Thee, Almighty God, command these things to be carried by the hands of Thy holy Angel to Thy Altar on high, in the sight of Thy Divine Majesty, that as many of us [*he kisses the Altar*] as, by participation at this Altar, shall receive the most sacred Body ✠ and ✠ Blood of Thy Son, may be filled with all heavenly benediction and grace Through the same Christ, &c. Amen.

COMMEMORATION OF THE DEAD.

Be mindful, O Lord, of Thy servants and handmaids *N.*, who are gone before us with the sign of faith, and sleep in the sleep of peace.

Canon Missæ.

Orat aliquantulum pro iis defunctis, pro quibus orare intendit.

Ipsis, Domine, et omnibus in Christo quiescentibus, locum refrigerii, lucis et pacis, ut indulgeas, deprecamur. Per eumdem Christum, &c. Amen.

Percutiens sibi pectus, elata parum voce, dicit—

Nobis quoque peccatoribus famulus tuis, de multitudine miserationum tuarum sperantibus, partem aliquam et societatem donare digneris, cum tuis sanctis Apostolis et Martyribus: cum Joanne, Stephano, Matthia, Barnaba, Ignatio, Alexandro, Marcellino, Petro, Felicitate, Perpetua, Agatha, Lucia, Agnete, Cæcilia, Anastasia, et omnibus Sanctis tuis: intra quorum nos consortium, non æstimator meriti sed veniæ, quæsumus, largitor admitte. Per Christum Dominum nostrum.

Per quem hæc omnia, Domine, semper bona creas, sancti ✠ ficas, vivi ✠ ficas, bene ✠ dicis, et præstas nobis. Per ip ✠ sum, et cum ip ✠ so, et in ip ✠ so, est tibi Deo Patri ✠ omnipotenti, in unitate Spiritus Sancti, omnis honor et gloria.

V. Per omnia sæcula sæculorum. *R.* Amen.

Præceptis salutaribus moniti, et divina institutione formati, audemus dicere:

Pater noster, qui es in cœlis, sanctificetur nomen tuum: adveniat regnum tuum; fiat voluntas tua sicut in cœlo, et in terra. Panem nostrum quotidianum da nobis hodie; et dimitte nobis debita nostra, sicut et nos dimittimus

He prays for such of the dead as he intends to pray for.

To these, O Lord, and to all that rest in Christ, grant, we beseech Thee, a place of refreshment, light, and peace. Through the same Christ our Lord. Amen.

Here, striking his breast, and slightly raising his voice, he says—

And to us sinners, Thy servants, hoping in the multitude of Thy mercies, vouchsafe to grant some part and fellowship with Thy holy Apostles and Martyrs; with John, Stephen, Matthias, Barnabas, Ignatius, Alexander, Marcellinus, Peter, Felicitas, Perpetua, Agatha, Lucy, Agnes, Cecilia, Anastasia, and with all Thy saints: into whose company we beseech Thee to admit us, not considering our merit, but freely pardoning our offences. Through Christ our Lord.

By whom, O Lord, Thou dost always create, sanctify, ✠ quicken, ✠ bless, ✠ and give us all these good things. Through Him, ✠ and with Him, ✠ and in Him, ✠ is to Thee, God the Father ✠ Almighty, in the unity of the Holy Ghost, all honour and glory.

V. For ever and ever. *R.* Amen.

Instructed by Thy saving precepts, and following Thy divine institution, we presume to say:

Our Father, who art in Heaven, hallowed be Thy name: Thy kingdom come; Thy will be done on earth as it is Heaven. Give us this day our daily bread: and forgive us our trespasses

debitoribus nostris.   Et ne nos inducas in tentationem.

M. Sed libera nos a malo.

Sacerdos, submissa voce, dicit "*Amen,*" et prosequitur—

Libera nos, quæsumus, Domine, ab omnibus malis, præteritis, præsentibus, et futuris: et intercedente beata et gloriosa semper Virgine Dei Genitrice Maria, cum beatis Apostolis tuis Petro et Paulo, atque Andrea, et omnibus Sanctis, da propitius pacem in diebus nostris, ut ope misericordiæ tuæ adjuti, et a peccato simus semper liberi, et ab omni perturbatione securi. Per eumdem Dominum nostrum Jesum Christum Filium tuum, Qui tecum vivit et regnat in unitate Spiritus Sancti Deus.

Postea, clara voce, dicit—

V. Per omnia sæcula sæculorum.   *R.* Amen.
V. Pax ✠ Domini sit ✠ semper vobis ✠ cum.
R. Et cum spiritu tuo.

Dicit secrete—

Hæc commixtio et consecratio Corporis et Sanguinis Domini nostri Jesu Christi fiat accipientibus nobis in vitam æternam.   Amen.

Et, ter pectus percutiens, dicit—

Agnus Dei, qui tollis peccata mundi, miserere nobis (*bis*).

Canon of the Mass. 69

as we forgive them that trespass against us. And lead us not into temptation.

R. But deliver us from evil.

He then says in a low voice "Amen," and continues—

Deliver us, we beseech Thee, O Lord, from all evils, past, present, and to come; and by the intercession of the blessed and glorious Mary ever Virgin, Mother of God, together with Thy blessed Apostles Peter and Paul, and Andrew and all the Saints [*making the sign of the Cross on himself with the Paten, he kisses it, and says*], mercifully grant peace in our days, that by the assistance of Thy mercy we may be always free from sin, and secure from all disturbance. Through the same Jesus Christ Thy Son our Lord, Who with Thee in the unity of the Holy Ghost liveth and reigneth God.

Then he says aloud—

V. World without end. *R.* Amen.

V. May the peace of the ✠ Lord be ✠ always with ✠ you.

R. And with thy spirit.

In a low voice—

May this mixture and consecration of the Body and Blood of our Lord Jesus Christ be to us that receive it effectual to eternal life. Amen.

Striking his breast three times, he says—

Lamb of God, who takest away the sins of the world, have mercy upon us (*twice*).

Agnus Dei, qui tollis peccata mundi, dona nobis pacem.

In Missis pro Defunctis—

Dona eis requiem, dona eis requiem sempiternam.

Domine Jesu Christe, qui dixisti Apostolis tuis, Pacem relinquo vobis, pacem meam do vobis; ne respicias peccata mea, sed fidem Ecclesiæ tuæ; eamque secundum voluntatem tuam pacificare et coadunare digneris: qui vivis et regnas Deus, per omnia sæcula sæculorum. Amen.

Domine Jesu Christe, Fili Dei vivi, qui ex voluntate Patris, co-operante Spiritu Sancto, per mortem tuam mundum vivificasti; libera me per hoc sacrosanctum Corpus et Sanguinem tuum ab omnibus iniquitatibus meis, et universis malis, et fac me tuis semper inhærere mandatis, et a te nunquam separari permittas; qui cum eodem Deo Patre et Spiritu Sancto vivis et regnas Deus in sæcula sæculorum. Amen.

Perceptio Corporis tui, Domine Jesu Christe, quod ego indignus sumere præsumo, non mihi proveniat in judicium et condemnationem; sed pro tua pietate prosit mihi ad tutamentum mentis et corporis, et ad medelam percipiendam. Qui vivis et regnas cum Deo Patre, in unitate Spiritus Sancti Deus, per omnia sæcula sæculorum. Amen.

Genuflectit, surgit, et dicit—

Panem cœlestem accipiam, et nomen Domini invocabo.

Canon of the Mass. 71

Lamb of God, who takest away the sins of the world, grant us peace.

In Masses for the Dead—

Give them rest; give them eternal rest.

Lord Jesus Christ, who saidst to Thy Apostles: Peace I leave with you, My peace I give unto you; regard not my sins, but the faith of Thy Church; and vouchsafe to it that peace and unity which is agreeable to Thy will: who livest and reignest God for ever and ever. Amen.

Lord Jesus Christ, Son of the living God, who, according to the will of the Father, through the co-operation of the Holy Ghost, hast by Thy death given life to the world; deliver me by this, Thy most sacred Body and Blood, from all my iniquities and from all evils; and make me always adhere to Thy commandments, and never suffer me to be separated from Thee; who with the same God the Father and the Holy Ghost livest and reignest God for ever and ever. Amen.

Let not the participation of Thy Body, O Lord Jesus Christ, which I, unworthy, presume to receive, turn to my judgment and condemnation: but through Thy goodness may it be to me a safeguard and remedy, both of soul and body. Who with God the Father, in the unity of the Holy Ghost, livest and reignest God for ever and ever. Amen.

Making a genuflection, the Priest rises and says—

I will take the bread of heaven, and call upon the name of the Lord.

Deinde, percutiens pectus, elevata aliquantulum voce, dicit ter devote et humiliter—

Domine, non sum dignus ut intres sub tectum meum; sed tantum dic verbo, et sanabitur anima mea.

Postea dicit—

Corpus Domini nostri Jesu Christi custodiat animam meam in vitam æternam. Amen.

Sumit reverenter Hostiam, et quiescit aliquantulum. Deinde dicit—

Quid retribuam Domino pro omnibus quæ retribuit mihi? Calicem salutaris accipiam, et nomen Domini invocabo. Laudans invocabo Dominum, et ab inimicis meis salvus ero.

Accipiens Calicem, dicit—

Sanguis Domini nostri Jesu Christi custodiat animam meam in vitam æternam. Amen.

Sumit totum sanguinem cum particula. Quo sumpto, si qui sunt communicandi eos communicet antequam se purificat. Elevans particulam, dicit—

Ecce Agnus Dei, ecce qui tollit peccata mundi.

Et ter dicit Domine, non sum dignus, *&c. Tum unicuique porrigens sacramentum, dicit—*

Corpus Domini nostri Jesu Christi custodiat animam tuam in vitam æternam. Amen.

Canon of the Mass. 73

Then striking his breast, and raising his voice a little, he says three times—

Lord, I am not worthy that Thou shouldst enter under my roof; but only say the word, and my soul shall be healed.

After which he says—

May the body of our Lord Jesus Christ preserve my soul to life everlasting. Amen.

He then receives the sacred Host, and after a short pause, says—

What shall I render to the Lord for all He hath rendered unto me? I will take the chalice of salvation, and call upon the name of the Lord. Praising I will call upon the Lord, and I shall be saved from my enemies.

Receiving the Chalice, he says—

The Blood of our Lord Jesus Christ preserve my soul to everlasting life. Amen.

(Those who are to Communicate go up to the Sanctuary at the Domine, non sum dignus, when the Acolyth says the Confiteor.)
Then the Priest, turning to the communicants, pronounces the Absolution; and elevating a particle of the Blessed Sacrament, and turning towards the people, he says—

Behold the Lamb of God, behold Him who taketh away the sins of the world.

And then repeats three times, Domine, non sum dignus, &c.

He then administers the Holy Communion, saying to each—

May the Body of our Lord Jesus Christ preserve thy soul to life everlasting. Amen.

Canon Missæ.

Se purificans, dicit—

Quod ore sumpsimus, Domine, pura mente capiamus; et de munere temporali fiat nobis remedium sempiternum.

Abluens manus, dicit—

Corpus tuum, Domine, quod sumpsi, et Sanguis quem potavi, adhæreat visceribus meis : et præsta, ut in me non remaneat scelerum macula, quem pura et sancta refecerunt sacramenta. Qui vivis et regnas in sæcula sæculorum. Amen.

Extergit os et calicem, quem operit, et plicato corporali, collocat in Altari ut prius ; deinde, legit Communionem et versus ad populum dicit—

V. Dominus vobiscum.
R. Et cum spiritu tuo.

Tunc legitur Post Communio. Postea, versus ad populum, dicit—

V. Dominus vobiscum.
R. Et cum spiritu tuo.
Ite, missa est.
R. Deo gratias.

In Missis Defunctorum dicit—

Requiescant in pace. *R.* Amen.

Inclinans se ante Altare, dicit—

Placeat tibi, sancta Trinitas, obsequium servitutis meæ; et præsta ut sacrificium quod oculis tuæ Majestatis indignus obtuli, tibi sit acceptabile, mihique, et omnibus pro quibus

Canon of the Mass.

Taking the first ablution, he says—

Grant, Lord, that what we have taken with our mouth we may receive with a pure mind; and of a temporal gift may it become to us an eternal remedy.

Taking the second ablution, he says—

May Thy Body, O Lord, which I have received, and Thy Blood which I have drunk, cleave to my bowels; and grant that no stain of sin may remain in me, who have been refreshed with pure and holy sacraments. Who livest, &c. Amen.

He then wipes the Chalice, which he covers; and having folded the corporal, places it on the Altar, as at first; he then reads the Communion. Then he turns to the people, and says—

V. The Lord be with you.
R. And with thy spirit.

Then he reads the Post-Communions. Afterwards he turns again towards the people, and says—

V. The Lord be with you.
R. And with thy spirit.
Depart, the Mass is ended.
R. Thanks be to God.

In Masses for the Dead—

May they rest in peace. R. Amen.

Bowing down before the Altar, he says—

O Holy Trinity, let the performance of my homage be pleasing to Thee; and grant that the sacrifice which I, unworthy, have offered up in the sight of Thy majesty, may be accept-

illud obtuli, sit, te miserante, propitiabile. Per Christum Dominum nostrum. Amen.

Deinde osculatur Altare, et elevatis oculis, extendens, elevans, et jungens manus, caputque cruci inclinans, dicit—

Benedicat vos omnipotens Deus (*et versus ad populum benedicens prosequitur*), Pater, et Filius, ✠ et Spiritus Sanctus. Amen.

R. Amen.

*Benedictio non datur in Missis Defunctorum.
Deinde in cornu Evangeli, dicit—*

V. Dominus vobiscum.
R. Et cum spiritu tuo.

Et signans Altare et se, legit Evangelium secundum Joannem, dicens—

S. Initium sancti Evangelii secundum Joannem.

M. Gloria tibi, Domine.

In principio erat Verbum, et Verbum erat apud Deum; et Deus erat Verbum: hoc erat in principio apud Deum. Omnia per ipsum facta sunt, et sine ipso factum est nihil quod factum est: in ipso vita erat, et vita erat lux hominum; et lux in tenebris lucet, et tenebræ eam non comprehenderunt. Fuit homo missus a Deo, cui nomen erat Joannes. Hic venit in testimonium, ut testimonium perhiberet de lumine, ut omnes crederent per illum. Non erat ille lux: sed ut testimonium perhiberet de lumine.

Ordinary of the Mass. 77

able to Thee, and through Thy mercy be a propitiation for me, and all those for whom I have offered it. Through Christ our Lord. Amen.

Then he kisses the Altar, and raising his eyes, extending, raising, and joining his hands, he bows his head to the Crucifix, and says—

May Almighty God, the Father, Son, ✠ and Holy Ghost, bless you. Amen.

R. Amen.

At the word "Deus," he turns towards the people, and makes the sign of the cross on them. Then turning to the Gospel side of the Altar, he says—

V. The Lord be with you.
R. And with thy spirit.

(The *Benediction* is omitted in Masses for the Dead.)

He then begins the Gospel according to St. John, saying—

P. The beginning of the holy Gospel according to St. John.
R. Glory be to Thee, O Lord.

In the beginning was the Word, and the Word was with God, and the Word was God: the same was in the beginning with God. All things were made by Him, and without Him was made nothing that was made: in Him was life, and the life was the light of men; and the light shineth in darkness, and the darkness did not comprehend it. There was a man sent from God, whose name was John. This man came for a witness to give testimony of the light, that all men might believe through him. He

Ordo Missæ.

Erat lux vera quæ illuminat omnem hominem venientem in hunc mundum. In mundo erat, et mundus per ipsum factus est, et mundus eum non cognovit. In propria venit, et sui eum non receperunt. Quotquot autem receperunt eum, dedit eis potestatem filios Dei fieri: his qui credunt in nomine ejus, qui non ex sanguinibus, neque ex voluntate carnis, neque ex voluntate viri, sed ex Deo nati sunt. ET VERBUM CARO FACTUM EST [*hic genuflectitur*], et habitavit in nobis: et vidimus gloriam ejus, gloriam quasi Unigeniti a Patre, plenum gratiæ et veritatis.

M. Deo gratis.

PSALMUS 150.

Laudate Dominum in sanctis ejus: laudate eum in firmamento virtutis ejus.

Laudate eum in virtutibus ejus: laudate eum secundum multitudinem magnitudinis ejus.

Laudate eum in sono tubæ: laudate eum in psalterio et cithara.

Laudate eum in tympano et choro: laudate eum in chordis et organo.

Laudate eum in cymbalis benesonantibus: laudate eum in cymbalis jubilationis, omnis spiritus laudet Dominum.

Gloria, etc.

was not the light, but was to give testimony of the light. That was the true light which enlighteneth every man that cometh into this world. He was in the world, and the world was made by Him, and the world knew him not. He came unto his own, and His own received Him not. But as many as received Him, to them He gave power to become the sons of God: to those that believe in His name, who are born not of blood, nor of the will of the flesh, nor of the will of man, but of God. AND THE WORD WAS MADE FLESH [*here the people kneel down*], and dwelt among us; and we saw His glory, as it were the glory of the only-begotten of the Father, full of grace and truth.

R. Thanks be to God.

When a Feast falls on a Sunday, or other day which has a proper Gospel of its own, the Gospel of the day is read instead of the Gospel of St. John.

Praise ye the Lord in all His holy places: praise ye Him in the firmament of His power.

Praise ye Him for His mighty acts: praise ye Him according to the multitude of His greatness.

Praise Him with sound of trumpet: praise Him with psaltery and harp.

Praise Him with timbrel and choir: praise Him with strings and organs.

Praise Him on high-sounding cymbals: praise Him on cymbals of joy, let every spirit praise the Lord.

Glory, etc.

A METHOD OF HEARING MASS BY WAY OF MEDITATION ON THE PASSION.

The Priest begins Mass.

Son of the living God, who, being in prayer, wouldst be comforted by an angel, grant me, by the virtue of Thy prayer, that when I pray Thy holy angel may assist and comfort me. Amen.

Confiteor.

Lord Jesus Christ, who, praying in the garden unto Thy heavenly Father, being in agony, didst miraculously sweat blood from all Thy members; grant that by the remembrance of Thy bitter passion, I may shed tears of sincere repentance now in Thy presence. Amen.

The Priest kisses the Altar.

Lord Jesus Christ, who sufferedst Judas to betray Thee with a kiss; grant that I may never betray Thee in my neighbour or myself; nor ever return evil to my enemies, but the good offices of charity. Amen.

The Priest goes to the Epistle Side.

Lord Jesus Christ, who wouldst be bound by the hands of wicked men; loosen, I beseech Thee, the chains of my sins, and so tie me with the bonds of charity, and the cords of Thy commandments, that I may neither in thought, word, nor deed, offend Thee hereafter. Amen.

The Introit.

Lord Jesus Christ, who wouldst be brought bound to Annas as a malefactor by an armed band of wicked persons, give me grace, that by no malignant spirit or bad men, I be ever drawn to sin, but by the good Spirit led to the fulfilling of Thy divine will. Amen.

Kyrie Eleison.

Lord Jesus Christ, who sufferedst Thyself to be thrice denied by the prince of the Apostles, in the house of Caiphas, preserve me, I beseech Thee, from ill company, that I may suffer all worldly losses, and even death itself, rather than deny Thee once. Amen.

Dominus Vobiscum.

Lord Jesus Christ, who, mercifully looking back on Peter, didst cause him bitterly to weep for his offences, look on me, I beseech Thee, with an eye of Thy mercy, that I may with tears fully bewail my sins in Thy presence, and neither in word nor deed offend Thee. Amen.

The Epistle.

Lord Jesus Christ, who wouldst be brought to Pilate, and before him falsely accused; teach me to avoid the fallacies of the wicked, and profess Thy faith truly by good works. Amen.

Munda cor meum.

Lord Jesus Christ, who before Herod didst for my sake suffer the same allegations of crimes against Thee, without returning the least word to justify Thyself, grant that I may patiently bear the injuries of the wicked, and learn from Thee, O my divine Master, to be meek and humble of heart. Amen.

The Gospel.

Lord Jesus Christ, who wouldst be again sent back by Herod to Pilate, and by that means cause a reconciliation between them, grant me not to fear the designs of my enemies, but to profit by their persecutions and follow Thy example. Amen.

The Unveiling of the Chalice.

Lord Jesus Christ, who wouldst be despoiled of Thy garments, and stripped naked, and scourged for my sake; grant me, by a naked confession of my sins, to put off the old man with all his acts, and never to appear naked of virtue in Thy sight. Amen.

The Offertory.

Lord Jesus Christ, who for me wouldst be bound unto a pillar, and there cruelly whipped, give me grace willingly to bear the rods of Thy paternal correction, and never to scourge Thee more by my transgressions. Amen.

The Covering of the Chalice.

Lord Jesus Christ, who for my sake wouldst be so cruelly crowned with thorns, pierce me so thoroughly with the thorns of penance, that I may have a right to be crowned by Thee in heaven. Amen.

The Priest washes his fingers.

Lord Jesus Christ, Son of the living God, who, though pronounced innocent by the president Pilate, didst hear, without opening Thy divine lips, the outcries of the Jews to crucify Thee; grant that I may live innocently, and that the malice of others may not trouble me. Amen.

Orate, Fratres.

Lord Jesus Christ, who for me wouldst be shown unto the Jews, with the ensigns of their mockery on Thee; give me grace to fly the ostentation of vain-glory, and to submit to mockery and contempt for Thy sake. Amen.

The Preface.

Lord Jesus Christ, who didst for my sake vouchsafe to receive the sentence of death, even the death of the Cross; make me for Thy love not to fear the sentence of the most cruel death that the perverted judgments of men can pronounce against me, nor ever perversely to judge others. Amen.

The Memento for the Living.

Lord Jesus Christ, who for me didst bear on Thy own shoulders Thy Cross; make me ardently to embrace the cross of mortification, and for the love of Thee to bear it daily after Thee. Amen.

The Priest holds his hands over the Chalice.

Lord Jesus Christ, who, in that miserable journey wherein Thou travelledst to Thy torture, didst so lovingly admonish the women that wept over Thee to mourn for themselves; give me grace to shed tears of repentance, that with them I may wash away my sins, and become acceptable to Thee. Amen.

The Priest makes the sign of the Cross over the Oblation.

Lord Jesus Christ, who wouldst for my sake be nailed on the Cross, and to the same didst fasten the handwriting of sin and death that was against me; transfix, I beseech Thee, my body with Thy holy fear, that firmly adhering to Thy precepts, I may for ever be fastened with Thee to Thy Cross. Amen.

The Elevation of the Host.

Lord Jesus Christ, who wouldst be raised on the Cross, and in that manner exalted from the earth for my sake; raise me, I beseech Thee, from all earthly affections, that my soul may always live in heaven. Amen.

The Elevation of the Chalice.

Lord Jesus Christ, who from Thy saving wounds madest the fountain of Thy grace to flow to us; grant that so often as wrong desires or sinister affections assail me, I may presently recur to Thy wounds, and from them draw my remedy. Amen.

The Memento of the Dead.

Lord Jesus Christ, who, hanging on the Cross, didst implore Thy Father for all mankind, even Thy crucifiers; give me, I beseech Thee, the grace of humility and patience, that according to Thy word and example, I may love my enemies, and do good to those that hate me. Amen.

Nobis quoque peccatoribus.

Lord Jesus Christ, who didst so mercifully promise heaven to the thief that humbly acknowledged his injustice; behold me, I beseech Thee, with the same eyes of mercy, that now confessing my crimes, I may obtain pardon, and in the end of my life be strengthened with hope to be with Thee in heaven. Amen.

Pater Noster.

Lord Jesus Christ, who, amongst other words spoken by Thee on the Cross, didst recommend Thy Mother to Thy beloved disciple, and him again to her; I commend unto Thee myself and all that I have, with a firm faith and confidence in Thy protection, beseeching Thee that, by their intercession, Thou wouldst preserve me amidst the troubles and dangers of this life. Amen.

The Breaking of the Host.

Lord Jesus Christ, who for my sake, dying on the cross, didst commend Thy soul unto Thy Father; grant that in this life I may spiritually die with Thee, and in the hour of my death commend my soul unto Thee, who livest and reignest God, world without end. Amen.

The Priest puts part of the Host into the Chalice.

Lord Jesus Christ, who, after Thy glorious victory over the power of the devil, didst descend into Limbo, and tookest thence the souls of the Fathers, till then detained there: extend, I beseech Thee, the virtue of Thy most precious blood and passion to the faithful in Purgatory, that they may come to Thy eternal joys. Amen.

Agnus Dei.

Lord Jesus Christ, at whose patience in torments and blessed death, many beating their breasts lamented their offences; by Thy bitter passion and death, give me grace with my whole heart to grieve for my sins, and never to offend Thee more. Amen.

The Communion.

Lord Jesus Christ, who wouldst for my sake be buried in a new monument, give me, O Lord, my God, a new heart, that dying in Thee, I may happily participate in the glory of Thy resurrection. Amen.

The Ablution.

Lord Jesus Christ, who for me, miserable sinner, being dead, wouldst by Joseph and Nicodemus be embalmed with spices, and wrapt in white linen; grant me worthily to receive from Thy holy altar Thy true and living body in the Eucharist, and for ever conserve it in a clean heart and body. Amen.

After Communion.

Lord Jesus Christ, who didst, through Thy shut and sealed sepulchre, rise triumphant from the dead; grant me grace to rise from the bondage of sin, to walk in newness of life, that when Thou, who art my Judge, shalt appear, I may also appear with Thee in glory. Amen.

Dominus Vobiscum.

Lord Jesus Christ, who, after Thy resurrection, didst manifest Thyself to Thy beloved mother and disciples, to their great joy and consolation; mercifully grant me Thy grace that after this mortal life I may with them rejoice in Thy heavenly kingdom, enjoying Thy presence for ever. Amen.

The last Collect.

Lord Jesus Christ, who didst vouchsafe, after Thy resurrection, to converse forty days with Thy disciples, and instruct them in all the mysteries of faith; teach me, I beseech Thee, to live according to Thy doctrine, and never to swerve in the least from Thy will. Amen.

The last Dominus Vobiscum.

Lord Jesus Christ, who after the term of forty days didst ascend glorious into heaven, in the sight of Thy disciples; grant that my heart may, for Thy love, loathe all earthly things, attend only to eternal, and pant, hunger, and thirst after Thee. Amen.

The Gospel of St. John.

Lord Jesus Christ, who didst send the Holy Ghost upon Thy disciples, when they did continue praying; cleanse, I beseech Thee, my heart from all sin, that the same Holy Ghost may always dwell in it by His manifold gifts, and my soul be everlastingly comforted. Amen.

FOR THE HOLY SOULS IN PURGATORY.

Jesu! by that shuddering dread which fell on Thee;

Jesu! by that cold dismay which sickened Thee;

Jesu! by that pang of heart which thrilled in Thee;

Jesu! by that mount of sins which crippled Thee;

Jesu! by that sense of guilt which stifled Thee;

Jesu! by that innocence which girdled Thee;

Jesu! by that sanctity which reigned in Thee;

Jesu! by that Godhead which was one with Thee;

Jesu! spare these souls which are so dear to Thee;

Who in prison, calm and patient, wait for Thee;

Hasten, Lord, their hour, and bid them come to Thee,

To that glorious Home, where they shall ever gaze on Thee.

METHOD OF HEARING MASS BY SAINT LEONARD OF PORT MAURICE.

The Angelic Doctor, St. Thomas, tells us that we have all four special debts which we owe to Almighty God, answering to the four great ends for which Jesus Christ instituted the Holy Sacrifice of the Altar. These are :—

1. To praise and honour the infinite Majesty of God, in acknowledgment of His supreme dominion over us.

2. To satisfy Almighty God for the sins we have committed against Him.

3. To thank him for all the blessings He has bestowed upon us.

4. To implore His divine grace and assistance.

The method for hearing Mass here given is especially conformable to the spirit of the Church, whose wish it is that we should, when assisting at Mass, unite our intention to that of the priest, who offers up the Holy Sacrifice for the four ends just mentioned ; by so doing we shall be able, according to St. Thomas, to pay, in the most efficacious manner, the four debts which we have contracted with Almighty God.

As soon, therefore, as the Mass commences, while the Priest humbles himself at the foot of the altar, and says the *Confiteor*, make a short examination of conscience, an act of true contrition, beg pardon of God for your sins, and invoke the assistance of the Holy Spirit and of the Blessed Virgin, that you may hear Mass with all reverence and devotion.

Then divide the Mass into four parts, in which you will pay the four great debts, in the following way:—

ADORATION.

1. From the beginning to the Gospel you will pay your first debt of honouring and praising the Majesty of God, who is worthy of infinite honour and praise. Humble yourself, therefore, with Jesus; acknowledge your own nothingness; confess sincerely that you are but utter nothingness in the presence of His immense Majesty; and then with great modesty and recollection, with humility of heart and body, say—

O my God, I adore Thee, and acknowledge Thee to be the Lord and Master of my soul. I protest that all that I am, all that I have, I have from Thee; and since Thy exceeding Majesty demands an infinite homage and worship, and I, a miserable creature, am utterly unable to acquit myself of this great debt, I offer Thee the humiliations and the homage which Jesus offers to Thee upon the altar. That which Jesus does, I intend to do likewise, in union with Him. I humble and abase myself before Thy Majesty; I adore Thee with the humiliations of Jesus Himself; I rejoice and am full of joy that the blessed Jesus offers up to Thee for me an infinite honour and worship.

Close your book, and continue to make in your heart several acts of joy at the thought that God should be thus infinitely honoured; and say again and again—

Yes, my God, I rejoice at the infinite honour which this Holy Sacrifice gives to Thy Majesty; I delight in it; I rejoice as much as I know how, as much as I can.

Be not anxious to bind yourself to these words, but follow the promptings of your own devotion, keeping yourself recollected and united to God. In this way, how fully will you pay your first debt!

CONTRITION.

2. In the second part, which is from the Gospel to the Elevation, you will pay the second debt. Cast a glance upon your many grievous sins, consider the immense debt you have contracted with the Divine justice, and say with a humble heart—

Behold, O my God, the traitor who has so often rebelled against Thee! Alas! with deepest sorrow I hate and detest my grievous sins; and I offer Thee in satisfaction for them the satisfaction which Jesus gives Thee upon the Altar. I offer Thee all the merits of Jesus, the Blood of Jesus; Jesus, God and Man, who as a Victim is sacrificing Himself again for me; since upon that Altar my Jesus is my Mediator and my Advocate, by His most Precious Blood He is imploring pardon for me. I unite myself to the voice of that loving Lord; and I ask mercy for all my grievous sins. The Blood of Jesus cries to Thee for mercy; my sorrowful heart also cries to Thee for mercy. Ah, my beloved God, if my tears move Thee not, let the sighs of my Jesus move Thee; and that mercy which He obtained for all mankind upon the Cross, why should He not obtain it for me upon this Altar? Yes, I hope that, in virtue of that most Precious Blood, Thou wilt pardon me all my sins, which I will never cease to lament even to the last moment of my life.

Close your book, and repeat several times acts of true interior and earnest contrition. Give vent to your affections, and in silence, but in the depth of your heart, say to Jesus—

My beloved Jesus, give me the tears of Peter, the contrition of Magdalene, and the sorrow of those Saints who, once sinners, became afterwards true penitents, so that in this Mass I may obtain a complete pardon of all my sins.

Make many acts of this sort, with great recollection, and rest assured that you will thus most fully discharge all the debts which you have contracted by so many sins.

THANKSGIVING.

3. In the third part, which is from the Elevation to the Communion, consider the many and wonderful blessings you have received, and in exchange for them offer to Almighty God a gift of infinite value, the Body and Blood of Jesus Christ; invite all the Angels and all the Saints to thank Him for you in this or the like manner—

Behold me, my most loving God, laden with blessings, both general and particular, of body and soul, which Thou hast bestowed upon me, and which Thou wilt still bestow upon me, in time and in eternity. I see that Thy mercies towards me have been, and are, infinite. I am ready to pay Thee for them, even to the last farthing: wherefore, in gratitude and in payment for them, behold this Divine Blood, this most Precious Body, this innocent Victim, which I present to Thee by the hands of the priest. I know that this offering which I present to Thee is sufficient to pay Thee for the gifts Thou hast bestowed upon me. This gift of infinite value is of itself worth all the gifts which I have ever received, or ever shall receive, from Thee. Ye holy Angels, and all ye blessed Saints of heaven, help me to thank my God, and offer to Him, in thanksgiving for His blessings to me, not only this, but all the Masses which are at this moment being celebrated throughout the whole world; so that His loving-kindness may receive a complete recompense for all the blessings which He has given me, and which He will give me for ever and ever. Amen.

<small>Oh, how pleased is our good God with such a thanksgiving! Oh, how is He satisfied by this one offering, which, being of infinite value, is worth more than all other offerings put together! And in order to excite yourself the more to this devotion, invite the whole court of heaven to thank Him for you; invoke those Saints to whom you are more specially devout, and say to them in the inmost depths of your heart—</small>

O my beloved Saints and advocates, thank the goodness of God for me, that I may not live and die ungrateful; beg of Him to accept my good will, and to have regard to the loving thanksgivings which

Jesus in this Mass is offering to Him for me.

Do not be content with saying this once only, but repeat it again and again; and be assured that in this way you will completely acquit yourself of this great debt.

SUPPLICATION.

4. In the fourth part, which is from the Communion to the end of the Mass, after having made a spiritual communion while the priest is communicating sacramentally, consider God to be within you; open your heart, and ask Him for many graces, believing that Jesus then unites Himself with you, and prays for you: therefore, enlarge your heart, and do not ask for trifling things, but ask for great graces; for great is the offering which you make to God, namely, that of His Divine Son. Say, then, with a humble heart—

O my God, too well do I know how undeserving I am of Thy favours; I confess my exceeding unworthiness, and that for my many grievous sins I do not deserve to be heard by Thee. But how canst Thou refuse to listen to Thy Divine Son, who prays upon the Altar for me, and offers Thee His Blood and His Life? Hear, I beseech Thee, my most beloved God, the prayers of this my great Advocate, and for His sake grant me all the graces Thou knowest to be necessary for me to accomplish the great work of my eternal salvation.

And now I take courage to ask of Thee a general pardon for all my sins, and the grace of final perseverance. Moreover, I beg of Thee, O my God, trusting in the prayers of my Jesus, all virtues in an heroic degree, and all those efficacious aids which I require to become a Saint. I also ask of Thee the conversion of all unbelievers, and of all sinners, and particularly of those who are related to me either by ties of kindred or by spiritual affinity. I ask of Thee the deliverance, not of one soul only, but of all the souls in Purgatory; bring them all forth, so that, by the efficacy of this Divine Sacrifice, that prison of purification may remain empty. Convert the souls of all the living, so that this miserable world may become for Thee a paradise of delight, where we may love, reverence, and praise Thee in time until we come to praise and bless Thee for all eternity.

Ask then, ask for yourself, for your children, friends, and relations, ask that all your wants, both spiritual and temporal, may be supplied. Ask also for the fulness of all blessings upon the Holy Church, and for its deliverance from all evils; and ask, not with lukewarmness, but with great confidence, and be assured that your prayers, united to the prayers of Jesus, will be heard.

As soon as the Mass is over, make an act of thanksgiving to Almighty God; and leave the Church with a heart full of compunction, as if you were coming down from Mount Calvary.

FORM OF SERVING AT MASS.

The Server, kneeling at the left hand of the Priest, shall answer him as follows—

P. Introibo ad altare Dei.

S. Ad Deum qui lætificat juventutem meam.

P. Judica me Deus, et discerne causam meam de gente non sancta; ab homine iniquo et doloso erue me.

S. Quia tu es Deus fortitudo mea; quare me repulisti, et quare tristis incedo dum affligit me inimicus?

P. Emitte lucem tuam et veritatem tuam; ipsa me deduxerunt, et adduxerunt in montem sanctum tuum et in tabernacula tua.

S. Et introibo ad altare Dei; ad Deum qui lætificat juventutem meam.

P. Confitebor tibi in cithara, Deus, Deus meus; quare tristis es, anima mea, et quare conturbas me?

Form of Serving at Mass.

S. Spera in Deo, quoniam adhuc confitebor illi: salutare vultus mei, et Deus meus.

P. Gloria Patri, et Filio, et Spiritui Sancto.

S. Sicut erat in principio, et nunc, et semper, et in sæcula sæculorum. Amen.

P. Introibo ad altare Dei.

S. Ad Deum qui lætificat juventutem meam.

P. Adjutorium nostrum in nomine Domini.

S. Qui fecit cœlum et terram.

P. Confiteor Deo, &c.

S. Misereatur tui omnipotens Deus, et dimissis peccatis tuis, perducat te ad vitam æternam.

P. Amen.

S. Confiteor Deo omnipotenti, beatæ Mariæ semper Virgini, beato Michaeli Archangelo, beato Joanni Baptistæ, sanctis Apostolis Petro et Paulo, omnibus Sanctis, et tibi, Pater, quia peccavi nimis cogitatione, verbo et opere [*here he strikes his breast thrice*], mea culpa, mea culpa, mea maxima culpa. Ideo precor beatam Mariam semper Virginem, beatum Michaelem Archangelum, beatum Joannem Baptistam, sanctos Apostolos Petrum et Paulum, omnes Sanctos, et te, Pater, orare pro me ad Dominum Deum nostrum.

P. Misereatur vestri, &c.

S. Amen.

P. Indulgentiam, absolutionem, &c.

S. Amen.

When a Bishop says Mass, he here takes the maniple, which the Server must be ready to give him.

P. Deus tu conversus vivificabis nos.

S. Et plebs tua lætabitur in te.

P. Ostende nobis Domine misericordiam tuam.

S. Et salutare tuum da nobis.

P. Domine, exaudi orationem meam.

S. Et clamor meus ad te veniat.

P. Dominus vobiscum.

S. Et cum spiritu tuo.

P. Kyrie eleison.

S. Kyrie eleison.

P. Kyrie eleison.

S. Christe eleison.

P. Christe eleison.

S. Christe eleison.

P. Kyrie eleison.

S. Kyrie eleison.

Form of Serving at Mass. 103

P. Kyrie eleison.

P. Dominus vobiscum [*a Bishop says,* Pax vobis].

S. Et cum spiritu tuo.

P. Per omnia sæcula sæculorum.

S. Amen.

At the end of the Epistle, say,

Deo gratias.

The Epistle and Gradual being read, remove the book to the right hand of the Altar, making a reverence as you pass before the middle of the Altar. Let the Server ever kneel or stand on the contrary side to the book.

P. Dominus vobiscum.

S. Et cum spiritu tuo.

P. Sequentia sancti Evangelii secundum, &c.

Making the sign of the Cross, say—

S. Gloria tibi, Domine.

Make a reverence at the beginning and ending of the Gospel, and at the name of JESUS; and at the end say—

S. Laus tibi, Christe.

P. Dominus vobiscum.

S. Et cum spiritu tuo.

Here give the wine and water, and prepare the basin, water, and towel for the Priest. When the Priest has washed his fingers, kneel in your former place and answer—

P. Orate fratres, &c.

S. Suscipiat Dominus sacrificium de manibus tuis ad laudem et gloriam nominis sui, ad utilitatem quoque nostram totiusque Ecclesiæ suæ sanctæ.

P. Per omnia sæcula sæculorum.

S. Amen.

P. Dominus vobiscum.

S. Et cum spiritu tuo.

P. Sursum corda.

S. Habemus ad Dominum.

P. Gratias agamus Domino Deo nostro.

S. Dignum et justum est.

At *Sanctus, sanctus, sanctus,* &c., ring the bell.

And again, when you see the Priest spread his hands over the Chalice, go and kneel behind the Priest, and holding up the vestment with your left hand, and having the bell in your right, ring during the elevation of the Host, and presently do the same at the elevation of the Chalice. As often as you pass by the Blessed Sacrament, adore on your knees.

P. Per omnia sæcula sæculorum.

S. Amen.

P. Et ne nos inducas in tentationem.

S. Sed libera nos a malo.

P. Per omnia sæcula sæculorum.

S. Amen.

P. Pax Domini sit semper vobiscum.

S. Et cum spiritu tuo.

Form of Serving at Mass. 105

The Priest's communion being ended, be ready to give him, first wine, then wine and water. But if there be communicants, first say the *Confiteor*. Then remove the book to the left hand of the Altar, and return to your former place. [A Bishop here again washes his hands, as at the Offertory.]

P. Dominus vobiscum.

S. Et cum spiritu tuo.

P. Per omnia sæcula sæculorum.

S. Amen.

P. Dominus vobiscum.

S. Et cum spiritu tuo.

P. Ite, missa est, *or* Benedicamus Domino.

S. Deo gratias.

In Masses for the Dead—

P. Requiescant in pace.

S. Amen.

Remove the book, if it be left open; kneel and receive the Priest's blessing, answering—

Amen.

At a Bishop's Mass—

B. Sit nomen Domini benedictum.

S. Ex hoc nunc et usque in sæculum.

B. Adjutorium nostrum in nomine Domini.

S. Qui fecit cœlum et terram.

At the beginning of the last Gospel—

P. Dominus vobiscum.

S. Et cum spiritu tuo.

P. Initium, *or* Sequentia Sancti Evangelii, &c.

S. Gloria tibi, Domine.

At the end, say—

Deo gratias.

BENEDICTION OF THE BLESSED SACRAMENT.

Benediction is a devotion practised by the Church, in order to give adoration, praise, and blessing to God, for His infinite goodness and love, testified to us in the institution of the Blessed Sacrament, and to receive at the same time the Benediction or Blessing of our Lord there present.

When the Priest opens the Tabernacle, and incenses the Blessed Sacrament, is sung the hymn:

O salutaris Hostia,	O saving victim, opening wide
Quæ cœli pandis ostium :	The gate of heav'n to man below;
Bella premunt hostilia,	Our foes press on from every side;

Da robur, fer auxilium.	Thine aid supply, thy strength bestow.
Uni trinoque Domino	To thy great name be endless praise,
Sit sempiterna gloria,	Immortal Godhead, one in three!
Qui vitam sine termino	O grant us endless length of days
Nobis donet in patria.	In our true native land with thee.
Amen.	Amen.

LITANY OF THE BLESSED VIRGIN.

Kyrie eleison.
Kyrie eleison.
Christe eleison.
Christe eleison.
Kyrie eleison.
Kyrie eleison.
Christe, audi nos.
Christe, exaudi nos.
Pater de cœlis Deus,
Fili Redemptor mundi Deus, } *Miserere*
Spiritus Sancte Deus, } *nobis.*
Sancta Trinitas unus Deus,

Sancta Maria,
Sancta Dei Genitrix,
Sancta Virgo Virginum,
Mater Christi,
Mater divinæ gratiæ,
Mater purissima,
Mater castissima,
Mater inviolata,
Mater intemerata,
Mater amabilis,
Mater admirabilis,
Mater Creatoris,
Mater Salvatoris,
Virgo prudentissima,
Virgo veneranda,
Virgo prædicanda,
Virgo potens,
Virgo clemens,
Virgo fidelis,
Speculum justitiæ,
Sedes sapientiæ,
Causa nostræ lætitiæ,
Vas spirituale,
Vas honorabile,
Vas insigne devotionis,
Rosa mystica,
Turris Davidica,

} *Ora pro nobis.*

Turris eburnea,
Domus aurea,
Fœderis arca,
Janua cœli,
Stella matutina,
Salus infirmorum,
Refugium peccatorum,
Consolatrix afflictorum,
Auxilium Christianorum,
Regina Angelorum,
Regina Patriarcharum,
Regina Prophetarum,
Regina Apostolorum,
Regina Martyrum,
Regina Confessorum,
Regina Virginum,
Regina Sanctorum omnium,
Regina sine labe originali concepta,

} *Ora pro nobis.*

Agnus Dei, qui tollis peccata mundi,
Parce nobis, Domine.
Agnus Dei, qui tollis peccata mundi,
Exaudi nos, Domine.
Agnus Dei, qui tollis peccata mundi
Miserere nobis.

If the "Te Deum" be sung, the persons present stand until the words "Te ergo, quæsumus" ("We pray thee, therefore"), when they kneel.

Tunc sequitur hymnus *Tantum ergo Sacramentum;* dum cantantur verba *Veneremur cernui* ab omnibus persistendum est in inclinatione profunda (quæ tamen nunquam sit prostratio).

Tantum ergo Sacramentum
Veneremur cernui :
Et antiquum documentum
Novo cedat ritui ;
Præstet fides supplementum
Sensuum defectui.

Genitori, Genitoque
Laus et jubilatio,
Salus, honor, virtus quoque
Sit et benedictio :
Procedenti ab utroque
Compar sit laudatio.   Amen.

V. Panem de cœlo præstitisti eis. [Alleluia.]

R. Omne delectamentum in se habentem. [Alleluia.]

Oremus.

Deus qui nobis sub sacramento mirabili, passionis tuæ memoriam reliquisti ; tribue quæsumus, ita nos corporis et sanguinis tui sacra mysteria venerari ; ut redemptionis tuæ fructum in nobis jugiter sentiamus.   Qui vivis, &c.   Amen.

Then is sung the hymn *Tantum ergo Sacramentum;* all present making a profound inclination (not prostration) while the words *Veneremur cernui* are being said.

> Down in adoration falling,
> Lo! the Sacred Host we hail;
> Lo! o'er ancient forms departing
> Newer rites of grace prevail;
> Faith for all defects supplying
> Where the feeble senses fail.
>
> To the everlasting Father,
> And the Son who reigns on high,
> With the Holy Ghost proceeding
> Forth from each eternally,
> Be salvation, honour, blessing,
> Might and endless majesty!

V. Thou didst give them bread from heaven. [Alleluia.]

R. Containing in itself all sweetnesss. [Alleluia.]

Let us Pray.

O God, who hast left to us in this sacrament a memorial of Thy death and passion, grant us, we beseech Thee, so to venerate the mysteries of Thy Body and Blood that we may soon feel within ourselves the fruit of Thy redemption. Who livest and reignest, &c. Amen.

DEVOTIONS FOR CONFESSION.
PRAYERS BEFORE CONFESSION.

Jesus, bring back to my remembrance the sins and wickednesses by which I have offended Thee. Jesus, grant me the spirit of perfect penitence; that by contrition, confession, and satisfaction, I may obtain Thy grace and thoroughly cleanse my conscience.

Jesus, have mercy on me, a wretched sinner, whom Thou hast redeemed with Thy precious blood.

Jesus, Son of David, have mercy on me, enter not into judgment with Thy servants, for in Thy sight no man living shall be justified.

EXAMEN OF CONSCIENCE ON THE TEN COMMANDMENTS.

I. Have you wilfully entertained doubts against Faith, denied it, exposed it to danger by reading infidel or heretical books, been guilty of superstitious practices? Do you belong to any secret society? Have you despaired? presumed on God's mercy by culpably postponing your conversion? neglected your prayers? if so, how long?

Devotions for Confession.

II. Have you taken God's name in vain? Sworn uselessly? Perjured yourself?

III. Have you neglected to hear Mass on Sundays and days of obligation? done unnecessary servile work on such days? broken the abstinence or fasts? neglected your Easter duty?

IV. Have you been disobedient or disrespectful to parents or superiors, or neglected to take proper care of those under your charge?

V. Have you quarrelled, fought? desired revenge, borne ill-will? neglected to give alms?

VI., IX. Have you sinned against holy purity in thought, word, or deed? or caused others to do so? Have you been guilty of gluttony or intemperance?

VII., X. Have you stolen, cheated? How much? Given away what was not your own? neglected to make restitution? For how long? Have you opened or read letters not belonging to you?

VIII. Have you detracted or calumniated? How many? What injury have you done? what compensation is due? Have you told lies? betrayed secrets?

ACT OF CONTRITION.

O my God, I am heartily sorry for having offended Thee, and I detest my sins for love of Thee; I firmly resolve by Thy grace to sin no more. A contrite and humble heart, O God, Thou wilt not despise.

METHOD OF CONFESSION.

Kneeling down, make the sign of the Cross, saying—

In the name of the Father, and of the Son, and of the Holy Ghost. Amen.

Then ask a blessing in these words:

Pray, Father, give me your blessing, for I have sinned.

The Priest's Blessing:

May the Lord be in your heart, and on your lips, that you may, with truth and with humility, confess all your sins, in the name of the Father, and of the Son, and of the Holy Ghost. Amen.

Then say the first part of the Confiteor, as follows:—

I confess to Almighty God, to blessed Mary, ever a Virgin, to blessed Michael the Archangel, to blessed John Baptist, to the holy apostles Peter and Paul, to all the saints, and to you, father, that I have sinned exceedingly in thought, word, and

Method of Confession. 115

deed, through my fault, through my fault, through my most grievous fault.

Then say:

Since my last confession, which was [*mention how long since*], I accuse myself, &c.

After this, accuse yourself of your sins, either according to the order of God's commandments, or such other order as you find most helpful to your memory; adding, after each sin, the number of times that you have been guilty of it, and such circumstances as may very considerably aggravate the guilt; but carefully abstaining from such as are not pertinent or unnecessary, and from excuses and long narrations.

After you have confessed all that you can remember conclude with this or the like form:—

For these and all other my sins, which I cannot at present call to my remembrance, I am heartily sorry, purpose amendment for the future, and most humbly ask pardon of God, and penance and absolution of you, my ghostly father.

Therefore I beseech the blessed Mary, ever Virgin, blessed Michael the Archangel, blessed John Baptist, the holy apostles Peter and Paul, all the saints, and you, father, to pray to the Lord our God for me.

Then give attentive ear to the instructions and advice of your confessor, and humbly accept of the penance enjoined by him.

Whilst the Priest gives you absolution, bow down your head with great humility, call upon God for mercy, and repeat once again the *Act of Contrition*.

ABSOLUTIONIS FORMA.

Si pœnitens absolvendus sit, injuncta ei prius et ab eo acceptata salutari pœnitentia, primo dicit sacerdos—

Misereatur tui omnipotens Deus, et dimissis peccatis tuis, perducat te ad vitam æternam. Amen.

Deinde, dextera versus pœnitentem elevata, dicit—

Indulgentiam, absolutionem, et remissionem peccatorum tribuat tibi omnipotens et misericors Dominus. Amen.

Dominus noster Jesus Christus te absolvat, et ego auctoritate ipsius te absolvo ab omni vinculo excommunicationis (suspensionis), et interdicti, in quantum possum, et tu indiges.

Deinde: Ego te absolvo a peccatis tuis, in nomine Patris ✠, et Filii, et Spiritus Sancti. Amen.

Si pœnitens sit laicus, omittitur verbum "suspensionis."

Passio Domini nostri Jesu Christi, merita beatæ Mariæ Virginis, et omnium Sanctorum, quidquid boni feceris, aut mali sustinueris, sint tibi in remissionem peccatorum, in augmentum gratiæ, et præmium vitæ æternæ. Amen.

THE FORM OF ABSOLUTION.

When the Priest desires to absolve a penitent, a salutary penance having been first enjoined upon him, and accepted by him, he says first—

May Almighty God have mercy on thee, forgive thee thy sins, and bring thee to life everlasting. Amen.

Then, with his hand raised towards the penitent, he says:

May the Almighty and merciful Lord grant thee pardon, absolution, and remission of all thy sins. Amen.

May our Lord Jesus Christ absolve thee; and I by his authority absolve thee from every bond of excommunication (suspension), and interdict, as far as I am able, and thou needest.

Then I absolve thee from thy sins, in the Name of the Father ✠, and of the Son, and of the Holy Ghost. Amen.

If the penitent be a lay person, the word "suspension" is omitted.

May the Passion of our Lord Jesus Christ, the merits of the Blessed Virgin Mary, and of all the Saints, whatever good thou shalt do, or evil thou shalt sustain, be to thee for the remission of sins, for the increase of grace, and the reward of eternal life. Amen.

AFTER CONFESSION.

What thanks are not due to Thee, O my Jesus, for Thy great goodness to me? When I was faithless to Thy goodness and loving kindness, Thou hast had patience with me; and even when I offended Thee, Thy grace waited for me. It is to Thy infinite grace and goodness that I am indebted for this sacrament, in which Thou hast reconciled me to Thyself. To Thee, and to Thy precious blood, I desire to offer all the love of my heart, just cleansed from sin. Humbled before Thee, I cried out like David, Have mercy on me, O God, according to Thy great mercy; and Thou hast heard my prayer; O my God, Thou hast forgiven me my sins, Thou hast restored unto me the joy of Thy salvation. Join with me, O my dear Mother Mary, and you, my Angel Guardian and holy Patron, in thanking our dear Jesus for His goodness and mercy to me.

Accept, O Lord, I beseech Thee, this my confession, and mercifully pardon all my deficiencies, that, according to the greatness of Thy mercy, I may be fully and perfectly absolved in heaven; who livest and reignest with the Father and the Holy Ghost, &c.

FOR PERSEVERANCE.

Grant, O my Lord Jesus, that I may persevere in good purposes, and in Thy holy service till my death, and that I may this day begin in earnest, for all I have hitherto done is as nothing.

BEFORE COMMUNION.
DIRECT YOUR INTENTION.

O Lord Jesus Christ, King of everlasting glory, behold I desire to come to Thee this day, and to receive Thy body and blood in this heavenly sacrament for Thy honour and glory and the good of my soul, and [*here name any special intention*].

AN ACT OF FAITH.

I most firmly believe, O Jesus, that in this holy sacrament Thou art present verily and indeed; that here is Thy body and blood, Thy soul and Thy divinity. I believe that Thou, my Saviour, true God and true Man, art really here, with all Thy treasures; that here Thou communicatest

Thyself to us, makest us partakers of the
fruit of Thy passion, and givest us a pledge
of eternal life. I believe there cannot be a
greater happiness than to receive Thee
worthily, nor a greater misery than to
receive Thee unworthily. All this I most
steadfastly believe, because it is what Thou
hast taught us by Thy Church.

ACT OF CONTRITION.

O my God, I am heartily sorry for
having offended Thee, and I detest my sins
for love of Thee. I firmly resolve by Thy
grace to sin no more; a contrite and
humble heart, O God, Thou wilt not
despise.

HUMBLY BEG GOD'S GRACE.

O my God, Thou knowest my great
poverty and misery, and that of myself I
can do nothing: Thou knowest how unworthy I am of this infinite favour, and
that Thou alone canst make me worthy.
Since Thou art so good as to invite me thus
to Thyself, add this one bounty more to all
the rest: to prepare me for Thyself.
Cleanse my soul from its stains; clothe it
with the nuptial garment of charity; adorn

it with all virtues, and make it a fit abode for Thee. Drive sin and the devil far from this dwelling, which Thou art here pleased to choose for Thyself, and make me one according to Thy own heart; that this heavenly visit, which Thou designest for my salvation, may not, by my unworthiness, be perverted to my own damnation. Never let me be guilty of Thy body and blood by an unworthy communion. For the sake of this same precious blood, which Thou hast shed for me; deliver me, O Jesus, from so great an evil.

PRAYER OF ST. THOMAS AQUINAS.

O Almighty and Everlasting God, behold I draw near to the Sacrament of Thine only-begotten Son, our Lord Jesus Christ. I draw near, as a sick man to the physician of life, as one defiled to the Fountain of mercy, as one blind to the Light of the eternal splendour, as one poor and needy to the Lord of heaven and earth. Wherefore, I implore the fulness of Thine infinite bounty, that Thou wouldst vouchsafe to heal all my sickness, to wash away my defilement, to give light to my blindness, to enrich my poverty, and to clothe my nakedness, so that I may receive the Bread of Angels, the King of kings, and Lord of lords, with such contrition and devotion, such purity and faith, such purpose and intention, as may avail to the welfare and salvation of my soul. Grant me, I beseech Thee, to receive not only the Sacrament of the Body and Blood of my Lord, but also the very reality and power of the Sacrament. O most gracious God, grant me so to receive the Body of Thine only-begotten Son our Lord Jesus Christ, that very Body which He took of the Virgin Mary, that I may be truly incorporated into His mystical Body, and so numbered amongst its members. O most loving Father, grant me at last to behold face to face and for evermore the same Thy beloved Son, whom I purpose to receive now in my pilgrimage beneath the veils of the Sacrament. Who liveth and reigneth, &c. Amen.

Implore the prayers of the Blessed Virgin and of the Saints.

O all ye blessed Angels and Saints of God, who see Him face to face; and especially thou, Mary, ever-blessed Virgin,

Before Communion.

Mother of my God and Saviour Jesus Christ; I most humbly beg the assistance of your prayers and intercession, that I may in such manner receive Him here, in this place of banishment, as to be brought one day to enjoy Him with you in our true country, there to praise Him and love Him for ever.

Before Receiving.

God, be merciful to me a sinner.

Wash me and I shall be whiter than snow.

Cleanse my conscience and my thoughts, I beseech Thee, O God.

Set a watch before my mouth and guard the door of my lips.

O let not my heart be inclined to anything that is wrong.

To receive Communion, open the mouth, letting the tongue touch the inner side of the lip, and having received the Sacred Particle on the tongue, swallow it as soon as you can, to avoid all irreverent touching of the Sacred Host with the teeth or lips. Do not fix your eyes on the Priest or elsewhere, but occupy yourself with devout aspirations of the heart. Imagine that you receive the Sacred Host from the hands of Our Lady, or of Our Blessed Lord Himself.

ASPIRATIONS AFTER COMMUNION.

Behold, O Lord, I have Thee now, who hast all things. I possess Thee, who possessest all things, and who canst do all things: take off my heart then, O my God and my All, from all other things but Thee, for in them there is nothing but vanity and affliction of spirit. Let my heart be fixed on Thee alone; let me ever repose in Thee, for in Thee is my treasure, in Thee is the sovereign truth, true happiness, and a blessed eternity.

Let my soul, O Lord, feel the sweetness of Thy presence. Let me taste how sweet Thou art, O Lord! that, being allured by Thy love, I may never more run after worldly pleasures; for Thou art the joy of my heart, and my portion for ever.

Thou art the Physician of my soul, who healest all our infirmities by Thy Sacred Blood. I am that sick man, whom Thou camest from heaven to heal: oh, heal my soul, for I have sinned against Thee.

O true Light, which enlightenest every man that cometh into this world, enlighten my eyes, that I may never sleep in death.

O King of heaven and earth, rich in

mercy, behold I am poor and needy: Thou knowest what I stand most in need of; Thou alone canst assist and enrich me. Help me, O God, and out of the treasures of Thy bounty succour my needy soul.

O my Lord and my God, behold I am Thy servant; give me understanding, and excite my affections, that I may know and do Thy will.

Thou art the Lamb of God, the Lamb without spot, who takest away the sins of the world: oh, take away from me whatever may hurt me and displease Thee, and give me what Thou knowest to be pleasing to Thee and profitable to myself.

O my God and my All, may the sweet flame of Thy love consume my soul, that so I may die to the world for the love of Thee, who hast vouchsafed to die upon the cross for the love of me.

Stay with me O, Lord, stay with me, for the day is far spent and the evening draws near; stay with me, I beseech Thee, for I have yet a thousand woes to expose to Thee, my Adorable Saviour; to Thee, who art my Lord, and the only sincere friend of my soul.

ANIMA CHRISTI.

Anima Christi, sanctifica me;
Corpus Christi, salva me;
Sanguis Christi, inebria me;
Aqua lateris Christi, lava me;
Passio Christi, conforta me;
O bone Jesu, exaudi me;
Intra vulnera tua absconde me;
Ne permittas me separari a te;
Ab hoste maligno, defende me
In hora mortis meæ, voca me;
Et jube me, venire ad te,
Ut cum sanctis tuis laudem te,
In sæcula sæculorum.   Amen.

AVE VERUM.

Ave verum corpus, natum
Ex Maria Virgine;
Vere passum, immolatum
In cruce pro homine;
Cujus latus perforatum
Vero fluxit sanguine;
Esto nobis prægustatum
Mortis in examine.
O clemens, O pie,
O dulcis Jesu, Fili Mariæ.

SOUL OF CHRIST.

Soul of Christ, be my sanctification;
Body of Christ, be my salvation;
Blood of Christ, fill all my veins;
Water of Christ's side, wash out my stains;
Passion of Christ, my comfort be;
O good Jesu, listen to me;
In Thy wounds I fain would hide,
Ne'er to be parted from thy side;
Guard me, should the foe assail me;
Call me when my life shall fail me;
Bid me come to Thee above,
With Thy Saints to sing Thy love,
World without end.   Amen.

300 days at any time; seven years after Communion.

AVE VERUM.

Hail to Thee, true body sprung
From the Virgin Mary's womb,
The same that on the cross was hung,
And bore for man the bitter doom;
Thy whole side was pierced, and flowed
Both with water and with blood;
Suffer us to taste of Thee,
In our life's last agony.
O kind, O loving one,
O sweet Jesu, Mary's Son.

PRAYER.

To which is annexed a plenary indulgence, applicable to the souls in purgatory, which all the faithful may obtain, who, after having confessed their sins with contrition, received the Holy Communion, and prayed for the intentions of the Sovereign Pontiff, shall devoutly recite it before an image or representation of Christ crucified.

Behold, O kind and most sweet Jesus, I cast myself upon my knees in Thy sight, and with the most fervent desire of my soul I pray and beseech Thee that Thou wouldst impress upon my heart lively sentiments of faith, hope, and charity, with true repentance for my sins, and a firm desire of amendment, whilst with deep affection and grief of soul I ponder within myself, and mentally contemplate thy five most precious wounds; having before my eyes that which David spake in prophecy: "They have pierced My hands and My feet; they have numbered all My bones."

FIVE ACTS TO BE MADE BEFORE OR AFTER COMMUNION.

1. I detest and loathe all and each of my sins, and the sins of all other creatures, committed from the beginning of the world down to this hour, or that ever shall be committed; and, if I could, I would prevent them with God's grace, which I now invoke.

2. I praise and honour all good works, past or future, and I would, were I able with God's grace, which I now implore, multiply them again and again.

3. I intend to act, speak, and think to the greater glory of God, in union with all the holy intentions that the Saints have ever formed, or shall form.

4. I pardon and forgive from my heart all my enemies, all who calumniate or detract me, all who in any way injure me or wish me evil.

5. I would that I could save all men by dying for each. I would willingly do so with God's grace, which I now therefore humbly implore, and without which I can do nothing.

VARIOUS PRAYERS.

OF PARENTS FOR THEIR CHILDREN.

O Heavenly Father, I commend my children unto Thee. Be Thou their God and Father; and mercifully supply whatever is wanting in me, through frailty or negligence. Strengthen them to overcome the corruptions of the world, to resist the solicitations of evil, whether from within or without; and deliver them from the secret snares of the enemy. Pour Thy grace into their hearts, and confirm and multiply in them the gifts of Thy Holy Spirit, that they may daily grow in grace, and in the knowledge of our Lord Jesus Christ; and so, faithfully serving Thee here, may come to rejoice before Thee hereafter; through the merits of the same our Lord Jesus Christ, who with Thee and the Holy Ghost liveth and reigneth. Amen.

FOR DOING GOD'S WILL.

Each day do I ask of Thee, O Lord, that Thy will may be done on earth as it is in heaven. Hearken to my prayer, I beseech Thee, and grant that I may perform all my actions in compliance with Thy holy will, and ever make it the sole rule of my conduct. Deliver my soul from the slavery of its passions. Grant that they may all yield to Thy empire, and that to please and love Thee may ever be the predominant desire of my soul. Amen.

TO THE SAINT OF OUR NAME, OR PATRON.

O Blessed Saint *N.*, glorious citizen of heaven, as I render most humble thanks to God for all the good He hath done thee, so I beseech thee to remember me in thy prayers, and obtain for me the entire remission of my sins, the amendment of my life, and the imitation of thy good spirit and holy graces, that I may be perfectly reconciled to my Saviour, and always please Him; but especially I recommend to thee the hour of my death, that, by thy holy intercession, my soul may depart this world in the grace of God, and immediately come to life everlasting. Amen.

TO THE HOLY GHOST.

Come, O Holy Spirit! enlighten the minds of all with Thy sacred light, and inflame their hearts with the fire of Thy love. Teach us what we are to believe, and lead us to practise it. For, alas! what will it avail us to know what is required of us in order to be saved, if we do not endeavour to reduce it to practice?

CHAPLET RECOMMENDED BY ST. PHILIP.

Virgin Mary, Mother of God, pray to Jesus for me.

Or, Pray to Jesus, Thy Son, for me a sinner.

Or simply, Virgin and Mother.

Repeat either of these ejaculations sixty-three times in form of a Rosary.

PRAYERS OF ST. JOHN FRANCIS REGIS TO OUR BLESSED LADY FOR PURITY.

My Queen and my Mother! to thee I offer myself without any reserve: and to give thee a mark of my devotion, I consecrate to thee during this day my eyes, my ears, my mouth, my heart, and my whole person: Since I belong to thee, O my good Mother! preserve and defend me as thy property and possession. Amen.

ASPIRATION IN ANY TEMPTATION.

O Domina mea! O Mater mea! memento me esse tuum. Serva me, defende me ut rem et possessionem tuam. *Ave Maria.*

My Queen and my Mother! remember that I belong to thee: keep me, guard me as thy property and possession. Amen. *Hail Mary.*

[100 *days.*

AVE MARIA.

Prayer, "O Mary, conceived without stain," etc., to obtain a good death.

O Mary, conceived without stain, pray for us who fly to thee. Refuge of sinners, Mother of those who are in their agony, leave us not in the hour of our death, but obtain for us perfect sorrow, sincere contrition, remission of our sins, a worthy reception of the most holy Viaticum, the strengthening of the Sacrament of Extreme Unction, so that we may be able to stand with safety before the throne of the just but merciful Judge, our God and our Redeemer. Amen. [100 *days once a day.*

BEFORE A PICTURE OR MEDAL OF THE SACRED HEART.

Oh! Sacred Heart of Jesus, I implore
That I may love Thee daily more and more.
[300 *days.*

It is a pious custom observed by some Catholics to trace on their forehead these four letters, *I.N.R.I.* [*Jesus Nazarenus Rex Judæórum*] saying—

May Jesus Christ, my King, preserve me from a sudden and unprepared death. Amen.

IN ANY TIME OF TRIAL.

O most compassionate Jesus! Thou alone art our salvation, our life, and our resurrection. We implore Thee, therefore, do not forsake us in our needs and afflictions; but, by the agony of Thy most Sacred Heart, and by the sorrows of Thy immaculate Mother, succour Thy servants whom Thou hast redeemed by Thy most precious blood. [100 *days once a day.*

FOR THE POPE.

V. Let us pray for our Pontiff, *N.*

R. The Lord preserve him, and give him life, and make him blessed upon earth, and deliver him not up to the will of his enemies.

Pater noster. Ave Maria.
[300 *days once a day.*

FOR PURITY OF INTENTION.

Take from me, O my God, all vainglorious thoughts, all desire of praise, all envy, covetousness, gluttony, sloth, and luxury, all froward affections, all desire of revenge and harm to others. Give me, O Lord, an humble, quiet, peaceable, patient, tender, and charitable mind, and in all my thoughts, words, and deeds, to have a taste of Thy Holy Spirit.—*Prayer of Sir Thomas More.*

TO JESUS, GOD OF PEACE.

My heart sought peace in creatures, but it found none except in Thee, O Lord. O God of peace! my mind is disturbed, my heart is agitated, my passions rebel; say but the word and the storm will be appeased.

O sweet Jesus, Saviour of mankind, whose sacred body was fastened to the Cross with Three Nails, fix my heart to the same Cross with the Three Nails of Faith, Hope, and Charity.

PRAYER FOR THE SICK.

Divine Jesus, incarnate Son of God, who for our salvation didst vouchsafe to be born in a stable, to pass Thy life in poverty, trials, and misery, and to die amid the sufferings of the Cross, I entreat Thee, say to Thy Divine Father at the hour of my death: *Father, forgive him;* say to Thy beloved Mother: *Behold Thy son;* say to my soul: *This day thou shalt be with me in paradise.* My God, my God, forsake me not in that hour. *I thirst:* yes, my God, my soul thirsts after Thee, who art the fountain of living waters. My life passes like a shadow; yet a little while, and all will be consummated. Wherefore, O my adorable Saviour, from this moment, for all eternity, *into Thy hands I commend my spirit.* Lord Jesus, receive my soul. [300 *days.*

A PRAYER IN SICKNESS.

O sweet Jesus, I desire neither life nor death, but Thy most holy Will. Thee, O Lord, I look for; be it done unto me according to Thy pleasure. If Thou wilt, sweet Jesus, that I die, receive my soul; and albeit I come to Thee at the very evening, as one of the last, yet grant that with Thee and in Thee I may receive everlasting life. If Thou wilt, sweet Jesus, that I live on earth, I purpose to amend the rest of my life, and offer it all for a burnt-sacrifice unto Thee, for Thy honour and glory, and according to Thy blessed Will; and for the performing of this, I desire the assistance of Thy holy grace. Amen.

PRAYER FOR THOSE IN THEIR AGONY.

Most merciful Jesus, Lover of Souls! I pray Thee by the agony of Thy most Sacred Heart, and by the woes of Thy immaculate Mother, wash in Thy Blood the sinners of the whole world who are now in their agony, and who are this day to die. Amen.

Heart of Jesus, once in agony, pity the dying. [100 *days.*

VISIT TO THE MOST HOLY SACRAMENT.

O my Lord Jesus Christ, who through Thy love for mankind dost remain day and night in this Sacrament, all full of tenderness and love, expecting, inviting, and receiving all who come to visit Thee; I believe that Thou art present in the Sacrament of the Altar; from the abyss of my nothingness I adore Thee and give Thee thanks for all the benefits Thou hast conferred on me, and particularly that Thou hast given Thyself to me in this Sacrament and Thy most holy Mother Mary, to be my advocate; and also for having called me to visit Thee in this church. I salute Thy most Holy Heart this day, and this homage I direct to a threefold end: First, in thanksgiving for this great gift; secondly, in reparation for all the injuries Thou hast received from Thy enemies in this Sacrament; thirdly, I intend by this visit to adore Thee in those places throughout the world where Thou art least honoured and most neglected in this Sacrament. O my Jesus, with my whole heart I love thee; I regret I have so often grieved Thy infinite goodness. I propose for the future, with the assistance of Thy grace, never more to offend Thee. And as to the present, miserable though I am, I consecrate myself wholly to Thee; I give and make over to Thee my entire will, my affections, desires, all that I am. Henceforth do with me and all that is mine whatever it shall please Thee. One thing I ask of Thee, one thing I desire—Thy holy love, final perseverance, and the perfect accomplishment of Thy holy will. I commend to Thee the souls in Purgatory, especially those who have been most devout towards this most holy Sacrament and the most Blessed Virgin Mary. I also commend to Thee all poor sinners. In fine, O my dear Saviour, I unite all my affections to the affection of Thy most loving Heart; and thus united, I offer them to Thy Eternal Father, and beseech Him in Thy name, for love of Thee, graciously to accept them.

ITINERARIUM, OR PRAYERS FOR A JOURNEY.

Ant. In the way of peace.

Canticle of Zachary. Benedictus.

Blessed be the Lord God of Israel: because He hath visited and wrought the redemption of His people.

And hath raised up a horn of salvation to us : in the house of David His servant.

As He spoke by the mouth of His holy prophets : who are from the beginning.

Salvation from our enemies : and from the hand of all that hate us.

To perform mercy to our fathers : and to remember His holy testament.

The oath which he swore to Abraham our father : that He would grant to us :

That being delivered from the hand of our enemies : we may serve Him without fear,

In holiness and justice before Him : all our days.

And thou, child, shalt be called the Prophet of the Highest : for thou shalt go before the face of the Lord to prepare His ways.

To give knowledge of salvation to His people : unto the remission of their sins.

Through the bowels of the mercy of our God : in which the Orient from on high hath visited us.

To enlighten them that sit in darkness, and in the shadow of death: to direct our feet into the way of peace.

Prayers for a Journey.

Glory, &c.

Ant. In the way of peace and prosperity may the omnipotent and merciful Lord direct us; may the Angel Raphael accompany us on our way, that we may return to our home in peace, in safety, and in joy.

Lord, have mercy on us. Christ, have mercy on us. Lord, have mercy on us.

Our Father (secretly).

V. And lead us not into temptation.

R. But deliver us from evil. Amen.

V. Save thy servants.

R. Who hope in Thee, O my God.

V. Send us help, O Lord, from the sanctuary.

R. And defend us out of Sion.

V. Be unto us, O Lord, a tower of strength.

R. From the face of the enemy.

V. Let not the enemy prevail against us.

R. Nor the son of iniquity approach to hurt us.

V. Blessed be the Lord day by day.

R. May the God of our salvation render our journey prosperous.

V. Show unto us Thy ways, O Lord.

R. And teach us Thy paths.

V. Let our steps be directed.

R. To keeping the way of Thy commandments.

V. The crooked ways shall be made straight.

R. And the rough places smooth.

V. God hath given his angels charge over thee.

R. To keep thee in all thy ways.

V. O Lord, hear my prayer.

R. And let my cry come unto Thee.

Let us pray.

O God, who didst make the children of Israel to pass dryshod through the midst of the sea; and who by the leading of a star didst show to the three kings the way unto Thee: grant to us, we beseech Thee, a prosperous journey and a quiet time, that under the guidance of Thy holy Angel, we may happily arrive at the place whither we are going, and at length reach the haven of eternal salvation.

O God, who didst lead Abraham Thy servant out of Ur of the Chaldeans, and didst keep him unhurt through all the ways of his pilgrimage, vouchsafe, we beseech Thee, to keep us Thy servants; be unto us, O Lord, a help in our going forth, a solace on the way, a shade from the heat, a shelter from the rain and cold, a chariot in weariness, a defence in adversity, a staff in slippery places, a haven in shipwreck, that Thou being our Leader, we may prosperously reach the end of our journey, and at length return in safety to our home.

Give ear, we beseech Thee, O Lord, to our supplications, and dispose the way of Thy servants in the paths of Thy salvation, that amid all the changes of this journey and of this life, we may ever be protected by Thy aid.

Grant, we beseech Thee, Almighty God, that this Thy family may walk in the way of salvation, and following the counsels of blessed John Thy precursor, may safely attain to him whom he foretold, our Lord Jesus Christ, Thy Son, who liveth and reigneth with Thee in the unity of the Holy Ghost, God, world without end. Amen.

V. Let us proceed in peace.

R In the name of the Lord. Amen.

PRAYERS FOR A HAPPY DEATH.

O Lord Jesus, God of goodness and Father of mercies, I approach to Thee with a contrite and humble heart; to Thee I recommend the last hour of my life and the decision of my eternal doom.

When my feet, benumbed with death, shall admonish me that my mortal course is drawing to an end, *Merciful Jesus, have mercy on me.*

When my eyes, dim and troubled at the approach of death, shall fix themselves on Thee, my last and only Support, *Merciful Jesus, have mercy on me.*

When my face, pale and livid, shall inspire the beholders with pity and dismay; when my hair, bathed in the sweat of death, and stiffening on my head, shall forbode my approaching end, *Merciful Jesus, have mercy on me.*

When my ears, soon to be for ever shut to the discourse of men, shall be open to hear the irrevocable decree which is to cut me off from the number of the living, *Merciful Jesus, have mercy on me.*

When my imagination, agitated by dreadful spectres, shall be sunk in an abyss of

Prayers for a Happy Death. 145

anguish: when my soul, affrighted with the sight of my iniquities and the terrors of Thy judgments, shall have to fight against the angel of darkness, who will endeavour to conceal thy mercies from my eyes, and to plunge me into despair, *Merciful Jesus, have mercy on me.*

When my poor heart, exhausted by its frequent struggles, shall feel the pangs of death, *Merciful Jesus, have mercy on me.*

When the last tear, the forerunner of my dissolution, shall drop from my eyes, receive it as a sacrifice of expiation for my sins; grant that I may expire the victim of penance, and in that dreadful moment *Merciful Jesus, have mercy on me.*

When my friends and relations, encircling my bed, shall shed the tear of pity over me, and invoke Thy clemency in my behalf, *Merciful Jesus, have mercy on me.*

When I shall have lost the use of my senses, when the world shall have vanished from my sight, when my agonizing soul shall feel the sorrows of death, *Merciful Jesus, have mercy on me.*

When my last sigh shall summon my soul to burst from the embraces of the body, and to spring to Thee on the wings of impatience and desire, *Merciful Jesus, have mercy on me.*

When my soul, trembling on my lips, shall bid adieu to the world, and leave my body lifeless, pale, and cold, receive this separation as a homage which I willingly pay to Thy divine Majesty, and in that last moment of my mortal life, *Merciful Jesus, have mercy on me.*

When at length my soul, admitted to Thy presence, shall first behold with terror thy awful Majesty, reject me not, but receive me into Thy bosom, where I may for ever sing thy praises, and in that moment, when eternity shall begin to me, *Merciful Jesus, have mercy on me.*

Let us pray.

O God, who hast doomed all men to die, but hast concealed from all the hour of their death, grant that I may pass my days in the practice of holiness and justice, and that I may deserve to quit this world in the peace of a good conscience, and in the embraces of Thy love : through Christ our Lord. Amen.

A SHORT EXERCISE

IN PREPARATION FOR THE HOLY VIATICUM, AND WHICH MAY BE USED EVERY DAY.

1. My heart is ready, O God, my heart is ready; not my will, but Thine, be done. O my God, I resign myself entirely to Thee, to receive death at the time and in the manner it shall please Thee to send it.

2. I most humbly ask pardon for all my sins committed against Thy sovereign goodness, and repent of them all from the bottom of my heart.

3. I firmly believe whatsoever the holy Catholic Church believes and teaches; and by Thy grace, I will die in this belief.

4. I hope to possess eternal life by Thy infinite mercy, and by the merits of my Saviour Jesus Christ.

5. O my God, I desire to love Thee as my Sovereign Good, above all things, and to despise this miserable world. I desire to love my neighbour as myself, for the love of Thee, and to forgive all injuries from my heart.

6. O my divine Jesus, how great is my

desire to receive Thy sacred Body! Oh, come now into my soul, at least by a spiritual communion! Oh, grant that I may worthily receive Thee before my death! I desire to unite myself to all the worthy communions which shall be made in Thy holy Church, even to the end of the world.

7. Grant me the grace, O my Divine Saviour, perfectly to efface all the sins I have committed by any of my senses, by applying daily to my soul Thy blessed merits and the holy unction of Thy precious blood.

8. Holy Virgin, Mother of God, defend me from my enemies in my last hour, and present me to Thy Divine Son. Glorious St. Michael, prince of the heavenly host, and thou, my angel guardian, and you, my blessed patrons, intercede for me, and assist me, in this last and dreadful passage.

9. O my God, I renounce all the temptations of the enemy, and in general whatsoever may displease Thee. I adore and accept of Thy Divine appointments with regard to me, and entirely abandon myself to them as most just and equitable.

10. O Jesus, my Divine Saviour, be Thou a Jesus to me, and save me. O my God, hiding myself with an humble confidence in Thy dear wounds, I give up my soul into Thy divine hands. Oh! receive it into the bosom of Thy mercy. Amen.

PRAYER FOR THE DYING.

O God, the giver of pardon, and lover of man's salvation, grant, we beseech Thee, that of thy merciful clemency those who are in their agony and are to die this day may, by the intercession of the ever blessed Virgin Mary, and all the saints, attain to the fellowship of everlasting happiness.

PRAYERS IN TIME OF SUFFERING.

O Lord Jesus Christ, accept my sufferings which I desire to unite with Thine; sanctify this affliction, so that every pain I feel may purify my soul, and bring it nearer to Thee. O Lord Jesus Christ, I beseech Thee to give me such love for Thee, that I may love the very sufferings that will take me sooner to Thee. Only stand Thou by me with Thy supporting grace, and then order for me what Thou pleasest. Amen.

MISERERE.
Psalmus 50.

Miserere mei, Deus :* secundum magnam misericordiam tuam.

Et secundum multitudinem miserationum tuarum :* dele iniquitatem meam.

Amplius lava me ab iniquitate mea : * et a peccato meo munda me.

Quoniam iniquitatem meam ego cognosco :* et peccatum meum contra me est semper.

Tibi soli peccavi, et malum coram te feci :* ut justificeris in sermonibus tuis, et vincas cum judicaris.

Ecce enim in iniquitatibus conceptus sum :* et in peccatis concepit me mater mea.

Ecce enim veritatem dilexisti :* incerta et occulta sapientiæ tuæ manifestasti mihi.

Asperges me hyssopo, et mundabor :* lavabis me, et super nivem dealbabor.

Auditui meo dabis gaudium et lætitiam :* et exultabunt ossa humiliata.

Averte faciem tuam a peccatis meis :* et omnes iniquitates meas dele.

MISERERE.

Have mercy on me, O God: according to Thy great mercy.

And according to the multitude of Thy tender mercies: blot out my iniquity.

Wash me yet more from my iniquity: and cleanse me from my sin.

For I know my iniquity: and my sin is always before me.

To Thee only have I sinned, and have done evil before Thee: that Thou mayest be justified in Thy words, and mayest overcome when Thou art judged.

For behold, I was conceived in iniquities: and in sins did my mother conceive me.

For behold, Thou hast loved truth: the uncertain and hidden things of Thy wisdom Thou hast made manifest to me.

Thou shalt sprinkle me with hyssop, and I shall be cleansed: Thou shalt wash me, and I shall be made whiter than snow.

To my hearing Thou shalt give joy and gladness: and the bones that have been humbled shall rejoice.

Turn away Thy face from my sins: and blot out all my iniquities.

Cor mundum crea in me, Deus : * et spiritum rectum innova in visceribus meis.

Ne projicias me a facie tua :* et spiritum sanctum tuum ne auferas a me.

Redde mihi lætitiam salutaris tui :* et spiritu principali confirma me.

Docebo iniquos vias tuas :* et impii ad te convertentur.

Libera me de sanguinibus, Deus, Deus salutis meæ :* et exaltabit lingua mea justitiam tuam.

Domine, labia mea aperies :* et os meum annuntiabit laudem tuam.

Quoniam si voluisses sacrificium, dedissem utique :* holocaustis non delectaberis.

Sacrificium Deo spiritus contribulatus :* cor contritum et humiliatum, Deus, non despicies.

Benigne fac, Domine, in bona voluntate tua Sion :* ut ædificentur muri Jerusalem.

Tunc acceptabis sacrificium justitiæ, oblationes, et holocausta :* tunc imponent super altare tuum vitulos.

Gloria, &c.

Miserere. 153

Create a clean heart in me, O God : and renew a right spirit within my bowels.

Cast me not away from Thy face: and take not Thy holy spirit from me.

Restore unto me the joy of Thy salvation : and strengthen me with a perfect spirit.

I will teach the unjust Thy ways : and the wicked shall be converted unto Thee.

Deliver me from blood, O God, Thou God of my salvation : and my tongue shall extol Thy justice.

O Lord, Thou wilt open my lips : and my mouth shall declare Thy praise.

For if Thou hadst desired sacrifice, I would indeed have given it: with burnt offerings Thou wilt not be delighted.

A sacrifice to God is an afflicted spirit : a contrite and humble heart, O God, Thou wilt not despise.

Deal favourably, O Lord, in Thy good will with Sion : that the walls of Jerusalem may be built up.

Then shalt Thou accept the sacrifice of justice, oblations, and whole burnt-offerings : then shall they lay calves upon Thine altar.

Glory, &c.

LITANY OF THE SAINTS.

Kyrie eleison.
Christe eleison.
Kyrie eleison.
Christe, audi nos.
Christe, exaudi nos.
Pater de cœlis Deus,
Fili Redemptor mundi Deus,
Spiritus Sancte Deus,
Sancta Trinitas unus Deus,
} *Miserere nobis.*

Sancta Maria,
Sancta Dei Genitrix,
Sancta Virgo virginum,
Sancte Michael,
Sancte Gabriel,
Sancte Raphael,
} *Ora pro nobis.*

Omnes sancti Angeli et Archangeli, *Orate, &c.*
Omnes sancti beatorum Spirituum ordines, *Orate, &c.*
Sancte Joannes Baptista, *Ora, &c.*
Sancte Joseph, *Ora, &c.*
Omnes sancti Patriarchæ et Prophetæ, *Orate, &c.*
Sancte Petre,
Sancte Paule,
Sancte Andrea,
} *Ora pro nobis.*

Litany of the Saints. 155

Lord, have mercy on us.
Christ, have mercy on us.
Lord, have mercy on us.
Christ, hear us.
Christ, graciously hear us.
God the Father of heaven, } *Have mercy on us.*
God the Son, Redeemer of the world,
God the Holy Ghost,
Holy Trinity, one God,
Holy Mary, } *Pray for us.*
Holy Mother of God,
Holy Virgin of virgins,
St. Michael,
St. Gabriel,
St. Raphael,
All ye holy Angels and Archangels,

All ye holy orders of blessed Spirits,

St. John Baptist,
St. Joseph,
All ye holy Patriarchs and Prophets,

St. Peter,
St. Paul,
St. Andrew,

Sancte Jacobe,
Sancte Joannes,
Sancte Thoma,
Sancte Jacobe,
Sancte Philippe,
Sancte Bartholomæe,
Sancte Matthæe,
Sancte Simon,
Sancte Thaddæe,
Sancte Mathia,
Sancte Barnaba,
Sancte Luca,
Sancte Marce,
Omnes sancti Apostoli et Evangelistæ,
Omnes sancti Discipuli Domini,
Omnes sancti Innocentes,
Sancte Stephane,
Sancte Laurenti,
Sancte Vincenti,
Sancti Fabiane et Sebastiane,
Sancti Joannes et Paule,
Sancti Cosma et Damiane,
Sancti Gervasi et Protasi,
Omnes sancti Martyres,
Sancte Sylvester,
Sancte Gregori,
Sancte Ambrosi,

} *Ora pro nobis, vel Orate pro nobis.*

Litany of the Saints.

St. James,
St. John,
St. Thomas,
St. James,
St. Philip,
St. Bartholomew,
St. Matthew,
St. Simon,
St. Thaddeus,
St. Mathias,
St. Barnabas,
St. Luke,
St. Mark,
All ye holy Apostles and Evangelists,
All ye holy Disciples of our Lord,
All ye holy Innocents,
St. Stephen,
St. Lawrence,
St. Vincent,
SS. Fabian and Sebastian,
SS. John and Paul,
SS. Cosmas and Damian,
SS. Gervase and Protase,
All ye holy Martyrs,
St. Sylvester,
St. Gregory,
St. Ambrose,

} *Pray for us.*

Sancte Augustine,
Sancte Hieronyme,
Sancte Martine,
Sancte Nicolae,
Omnes sancti Pontifices et Confessores,
Omnes sancti Doctores,
Sancte Antoni,
Sancte Benedicte,
Sancte Bernarde,
Sancte Dominice,
Sancte Francisce,
Omnes sancti Sacerdotes et Levitæ,
Omnes sancti Monachi et Eremitæ,
Sancta Maria Magdalena,
Sancta Agatha,
Sancta Lucia,
Sancta Agnes,
Sancta Cæcilia,
Sancta Catharina,
Sancta Anastasia,
Omnes sanctæ Virgines et Viduæ,
Omnes Sancti et Sanctæ Dei,

} *Ora pro nobis, vel Orate pro nobis.*

Intercedite pro nobis.
Propitius esto,
Parce nobis, Domine.
Propitius esto,
Exaudi nos, Domine.

Litany of the Saints. 159

St. Augustine,
St. Jerome,
St. Martin,
St. Nicholas,
All ye holy Bishops and Confessors,
All ye holy Doctors,
St. Anthony,
St. Benedict,
St. Bernard,
St. Dominic,
St. Francis,
All ye holy Priests and Levites,
All ye holy Monks and Hermits,
St. Mary Magdalen,
St. Agatha,
St. Lucy,
St. Agnes,
St. Cecilia,
St. Catherine,
St. Anastasia,
All ye holy Virgins and Widows,
} *Pray for us.*

All ye holy men and women, saints of God,
Make intercession for us.
Be merciful,
Spare us, O Lord.
Be merciful,
Graciously hear us, O Lord.

Ab omni malo,
Ab omni peccato,
Ab ira tua,*
A subitanea et improvisa morte,
Ab insidiis diaboli,
Ab ira, et odio, et omni mala voluntate,

A spiritu fornicationis,
A fulgure et tempestate,
A morte perpetua,
Per mysterium sanctæ Incarnationis tuæ,

Per Adventum tuum,
Per Nativitatem tuam,
Per Baptismum et sanctum Jejunium tuum,
Per Crucem et Passionem tuam,
Per Mortem et Sepulturam tuam,
Per sanctam Resurrectionem tuam,
Per admirabilem Ascensionem tuam,
Per adventum Spiritus Sancti Parācliti,
In die judicii,

} *Libera nos Domine.*

---

* Hic pro oratione XL. Horarum dicitur:

Ab imminentibus periculis,
A peste, fame, et bello.

Litany of the Saints.

From all evil,
From all sin,
From thy wrath,*
From sudden and unprovided-for death,
From the snares of the devil,
From anger, and hatred, and every evil will,
From the spirit of fornication,
From lightning and tempest,
From everlasting death,
Through the mystery of Thy holy Incarnation,
Through Thy Coming,
Through Thy Nativity,
Through Thy Baptism and holy Fasting,
Through Thy Cross and Passion,
Through Thy Death and Burial,
Through Thy holy Resurrection,
Through Thine admirable Ascension,
Through the coming of the Holy Ghost the Paraclete,
In the day of judgment,

} *O Lord, deliver us.*

---

* Here, for the Prayer of the Forty Hours, is inserted:
  From all dangers that threaten us,
  From plague, famine, and war,

Peccatores,
Te rogamus audi nos.
Ut nobis parcas,
Ut nobis indulgeas,
Ut ad veram pœnitentiam nos perducere digneris,
Ut Ecclesiam tuam sanctam regere et conservare digneris,
Ut Domnum Apostolicum, et omnes ecclesiasticos ordines in sancta religione conservare digneris,
Ut inimicos sanctæ Ecclesiæ humiliare digneris,*
Ut regibus et principibus Christianis pacem et veram concordiam donare digneris,
Ut cuncto populo Christiano pacem et unitatem largiri digneris,

Ut nosmetipsos in tuo sancto servitio confortare et conservare digneris,

Te rogamus audi nos.

---

* Pro Oratione xl. Horarum dicitur.

Ut Turcarum et hæreticorum conatus reprimere et ad nihilum redigere digneris.

Litany of the Saints. 163

We sinners,
Beseech Thee, hear us.
That Thou wouldst spare us,
That Thou wouldst pardon us,
That Thou wouldst bring us to true penance,
That Thou wouldst vouchsafe to govern and preserve Thy holy Church,
That Thou wouldst vouchsafe to preserve our Apostolic Prelate, and all orders of the Church in holy religion,
That Thou wouldst vouchsafe to humble the enemies of holy Church,*
That Thou wouldst vouchsafe to give peace and true concord to Christian kings and princes,
That Thou wouldst vouchsafe to grant peace and unity to all Christian people,
That Thou wouldst vouchsafe to confirm and preserve us in Thy holy service,

} *We beseech Thee, hear us.*

---

* For the Prayer of the Forty Hours, insert:
That Thou wouldst vouchsafe to defeat the attempts of all Turks and heretics, and bring them to nought.

Ut mentes nostras ad cœlestia desideria erigas,
Ut omnibus benefactoribus nostris sempiterna bona retribuas,
Ut animas nostras, fratrum, propinquorum, et benefactorum nostrorum ab æterna damnatione eripias,

Ut fructus terræ dare et conservare digneris,
Ut omnibus fidelibus defunctis requiem æternam donare digneris,

Ut nos exaudire digneris,

Fili Dei,
Agnus Dei, qui tollis peccata mundi,

Parce nobis, Domine.
Agnus Dei, qui tollis peccata mundi,

Exaudi nos, Domine.
Agnus Dei, qui tollis peccata mundi,

Miserere nobis.
Christe, audi nos.
Christe, exaudi nos.

Te rogamus audi nos.

Litany of the Saints.

That Thou wouldst lift up our minds to heavenly desires,
That Thou wouldst render eternal blessings to all our benefactors,
That Thou wouldst deliver our souls, and the souls of our brethren, relations, and benefactors from eternal damnation,
That Thou wouldst vouchsafe to give and preserve the fruits of the earth,
That Thou wouldst vouchsafe to grant eternal rest to all the faithful departed,
That Thou wouldst vouchsafe graciously to hear us,
Son of God,

} *We beseech Thee, hear us.*

Lamb of God, who takest away the sins of the world,
Spare us, O Lord.
Lamb of God, who takest away the sins of the world,
Graciously hear us, O Lord.
Lamb of God, who takest away the sins of the world,
Have mercy on us.
Christ, hear us.
Christ, graciously hear us.

Kyrie eleison.
Christe eleison.
Kyrie eleison.
Pater noster (*secreto*).
V. Et ne nos inducas in tentationem.
R. Sed libera nos a malo.

Psalm lxix. *Deus in adjutorium.*

Deus in adjutorium meum intende: Domine, ad adjuvandum me festina.

Confundantur et revereantur: qui quærunt animam meam:

Avertantur retrorsum, et erubescant: qui volunt mihi mala.

Avertantur statim erubescentes, qui dicunt mihi: Euge, euge.

Exultent et lætentur in te omnes qui quærunt te: et dicant semper, Magnificetur Dominus; qui diligunt salutare tuum.

Ego vero egenus et pauper sum: Deus, adjuva me.

Adjutor meus et liberator meus es tu: Domine, ne moreris.

Gloria Patri, &c.

V. Salvos fac servos tuos.
R. Deus meus, sperantes in te.

Litany of the Saints.

Lord have mercy on us.
Christ, have mercy on us.
Lord, have mercy on us.
    Our Father (*secretly*).
V. And lead us not into temptation.
R. But deliver us from evil.

    Psalm lxix.

O God, come to my assistance: O Lord, make haste to help me.

Let them be confounded and ashamed: that seek my soul.

Let them be turned backward, and blush for shame : that desire evils unto me.

Let them be presently turned away blushing for shame, that say unto me: 'Tis well, 'tis well.

Let all that seek Thee rejoice and be glad in Thee : and let such as love Thy salvation say always, The Lord be magnified.

But I am needy and poor: O God, help me.

Thou art my helper and my deliverer : O Lord, make no delay.

Glory be, &c.

V. Save Thy servants.
R. Who hope in Thee, O my God.

Litany of the Saints.

V. Esto nobis, Domine, turris fortitudinis.

R. A facie inimici.
V. Nihil proficiat inimicus in nobis.
R. Et filius iniquitatis non apponat nocere nobis.
V. Domine, non secundum peccata nostra facias nobis.
R. Neque secundum iniquitates nostras retribuas nobis.
V. Oremus pro Pontifice nostro, *N.*
R. Dominus conservet eum, et vivificet eum, et beatum faciat eum in terra; et non tradat eum in animam inimicorum ejus.

V. Oremus pro benefactoribus nostris.
R. Retribuere dignare, Domine, omnibus nobis bona facientibus propter nomen tuum vitam æternam. Amen.
V. Oremus pro fidelibus defunctis.
R. Requiem æternam dona eis, Domine; et lux perpetua luceat eis.
V. Requiescant in pace.
R. Amen.
V. Pro fratribus nostris absentibus.
R. Salvos fac servos tuos, Deus meus, sperantes in te.

Litany of the Saints.

V. Be unto us, O Lord, a tower of strength.

R. From the face of the enemy.

V. Let not the enemy prevail against us.

R. Nor the son of iniquity approach to hurt us.

V. O Lord, deal not with us according to our sins.

R. Neither requite us according to our iniquities.

V. Let us pray for our Sovereign Pontiff, *N.*

R. The Lord preserve him and give him life, and make him blessed upon the earth; and deliver him not up to the will of his enemies.

V. Let us pray for our benefactors.

R. Vouchsafe, O Lord, for Thy name's sake, to reward with eternal life all them that do us good. Amen.

V. Let us pray for the faithful departed.

R. Eternal rest give unto them, O Lord; and let perpetual light shine upon them.

V. May they rest in peace.

R. Amen.

V. For our absent brethren.

R. Save Thy servants, who hope in Thee, O my God.

V. Mitte eis, Domine, auxilium de sancto.

R. Et de Sion tuere eos.
V. Domine, exaudi orationem meam.
R. Et clamor meus ad te veniat.

*Oremus.**

Deus, cui proprium est misereri semper, et parcere: suscipe deprecationem nostram; ut nos, et omnes famulos tuos, quos delictorum catena constringit, miseratio tuæ pietatis clementer absolvat.

---

* Pro Oratione XL. Horarum sequentes preces dicuntur:
Deus qui nobis sub Sacramento mirabili, &c.
Concede nos famulos tuos, quæ sumus, Domine Deus, perpetua mentis et corporis sanitate gaudere; et gloriosa beatæ Mariæ semper Virginis intercessione, a præsenti liberari tristitia, et æterna perfrui lætitia.

Omnipotens, &c., pro Papa.
Deus, refugium nostrum et virtus, adesto piis Ecclesiæ tuæ precibus, auctor ipse pietatis; et præsta ut quod fideliter petimus, efficaciter consequamur.

Omnipotens sempiterne Deus, in cujus manu sunt omnes potestates, et omnia jura regnorum, respice in auxilium Christianorum, ut gentes paganorum et

Litany of the Saints. 171

V. Send them help, O Lord, from the sanctuary.

R. And defend them out of Sion.

V. O Lord, hear my prayer.

R. And let my cry come unto Thee.

*Let us pray.**

O God, whose property is always to have mercy and to spare, receive our humble petition; that we, and all Thy servants who are bound by the chain of sins, may, by the compassion of Thy goodness, mercifully be absolved.

---

* For the Devotion of the Forty Hours, the following Prayers are used:

Deus qui nobis sub Sacramento mirabili, &c.

Grant, we beseech Thee, O Lord God, that we, Thy servants, may enjoy perpetual health of mind and body; and, by the intercession of the Blessed Mary ever Virgin, may be delivered from present sorrow, and obtain eternal joy.

Omnipotens, &c., for the Pope, as above.

O God, our refuge and strength, who art the author of all piety, hearken unto the devout prayers of Thy Church; and grant that what we ask faithfully we may obtain effectually.

Almighty, everlasting God, in whose hand are all the powers and all the rights of kingdoms, come to the assistance of Thy Christian people, that all pagan

Exaudi, quæsumus, Domine, supplicum preces, et confitentium tibi parce peccatis: ut pariter nobis indulgentiam tribuas benignus et pacem.

Ineffabilem nobis, Domine, misericordiam tuam clementer ostende; ut simul nos et a peccatis omnibus exuas, et a pœnis, quas pro his meremur, eripias.

Deus, qui culpa offenderis, pœnitentia placaris: preces populi tui supplicantis propitius respice; et flagella tuæ iracundiæ, quæ pro peccatis nostris meremur, averte.

Omnipotens sempiterne Deus, miserere famulo tuo Pontifici nostro *N.* et dirige eum secundum tuam clementiam in viam

---

hæreticorum, quæ in sua feritate et fraude confidunt, dexteræ tuæ potentia conterantur.

Tunc sequitur ultima oratio, *Omnipotens sempiterne Deus, &c.*, cum versiculis, præterquam in penultimo responso loco simplicis Amen, dicitur—
R. Et custodiat nos semper. Amen.

Graciously hear, we beseech Thee, O Lord, the prayers of Thy suppliants, and forgive the sins of them that confess to Thee; that, in Thy bounty, Thou mayst grant us both pardon and peace.

Show forth upon us, O Lord, in Thy mercy, Thy unspeakable loving-kindness; that Thou mayst both loose us from all our sins and deliver us from the punishments which we deserve for them.

O God, who by sin art offended, and by penance pacified, mercifully regard the prayers of Thy people making supplication to Thee, and turn away the scourges of Thine anger, which we deserve for our sins.

Almighty, everlasting God, have mercy upon Thy servant, *N.*, our Sovereign Pontiff, and direct him according to Thy clemency into the way of everlasting salvation; that by Thy grace he may both desire those

---

and heretical nations, who trust in their own violence and fraud, may be broken by the might of Thy right hand.

Then follows the last Prayer, *Omnipotens sempiterne Deus, &c.*, *Almighty, everlasting God, &c.*, with the Versicles, except that, in the last response but one, &c., instead of the simple *Amen*, is said—

R. And ever preserve us. Amen.

salutis æternæ: ut te donante tibi placita cupiat, et tota virtute perficiat.

Deus, a quo sancta desideria, recta consilia, et justa sunt opera: da servis tuis illam, quam mundis dare non potest, pacem; ut et corda nostra mandatis tuis dedita, et hostium sublata formidine, tempora sint tua protectione tranquilla.

Ure igne Sancti Spiritus renes nostros et cor nostrum, Domine; ut tibi casto corpore serviamus, et mundo corde placeamus.

Fidelium Deus omnium Conditor et Redemptor, animabus famulorum famularumque tuarum remissionem cunctorum tribue peccatorum: ut indulgentiam, quam semper optaverunt, piis supplicationibus consequantur.

Actiones nostras, quæsumus, Domine, aspirando præveni, et adjuvando prosequere: ut cuncta nostra oratio et operatio a te semper incipiat et per te cœpta finiatur.

Omnipotens sempiterne Deus, qui vivo-

things that are pleasing to Thee, and perform them with all his strength.

O God, from whom all holy desires, all right counsels, and all just works do come, give unto Thy servants that peace which the world cannot give; that both our hearts being devoted to the keeping of Thy commandments and the fear of enemies being removed, our times, by Thy protection, may be peaceful.

Inflame, O Lord, our reins and heart with the fire of the Holy Ghost; that we may serve Thee with a chaste body, and please Thee with a clean heart.

O God, the Creator and Redeemer of all the faithful, give to the souls of Thy servants departed the remission of all their sins; that through pious supplications they may obtain that pardon which they have always desired.

Prevent, we beseech Thee, O Lord, our actions by Thy inspirations, and further them with Thy continual help; that every prayer and work of ours may always begin from Thee, and through Thee be likewise ended.

Almighty, everlasting God, who hast

rum dominaris simul et mortuorum omniumque misereris, quos tuos fide et opere futuros esse prænoscis; te supplices exoramus; ut pro quibus effundere preces decrevimus, quosque vel præsens sæculum adhuc in carne retinet, vel futurum jam exutos corpore suscepit, intercedentibus omnibus Sanctis tuis, pietatis tuæ clementia omnium delictorum suorum veniam consequantur. Per Dominum. R. Amen.

V. Dominus vobiscum.
R. Et cum spiritu tuo.
V. Exaudiat nos omnipotens et misericors Dominus. R. Amen.
V. Et fidelium animæ per misericordiam Dei requiescant in pace. R. Amen.

Litany of the Saints. 177

dominion over the living and the dead, and art merciful to all, whom Thou foreknowest will be Thine by faith and works; we humbly beseech Thee that they for whom we intend to pour forth our prayers, whether this present world still detain them in the flesh, or the world to come hath already received them stripped of their mortal bodies, may, by the grace of Thy loving kindness, and by the intercession of all the Saints, obtain the remission of all their sins. Through, &c. *R.* Amen.

V. The Lord be with you.

R. And with thy spirit.

V. May the Almighty and merciful Lord graciously hear us. *R.* Amen.

V. And may the souls of the faithful, through the mercy of God, rest in peace.

R. Amen.

THE ROSARY.

THE FIVE JOYFUL MYSTERIES.

I. The Annunciation.
II. The Visitation.
III. The Nativity.
IV. The Presentation.
V. The Finding in the Temple.

THE FIVE SORROWFUL MYSTERIES.

I. The Agony in the Garden.
II. The Scourging at the Pillar.
III. The Crowning with Thorns.
IV. Jesus carrying His Cross.
V. The Crucifixion.

THE FIVE GLORIOUS MYSTERIES.

I. The Resurrection.
II. The Ascension.
III. The Descent of the Holy Ghost.
IV. The Assumption.
V. The Coronation of our Blessed Lady

CORONA OR CHAPLET OF THE SEVEN DOLOURS OF OUR BLESSED LADY.

I. The Prophecy of Simeon.—One Our Father, seven Hail Marys.

II. The Flight into Egypt.—One Our Father, seven Hail Marys.

III. The loss of Jesus for three days.—One Our Father, seven Hail Marys.

IV. Her meeting Jesus carrying His Cross.—One Our Father, seven Hail Marys.

V. Her standing beneath the Cross on Calvary.—One Our Father, seven Hail Marys.

VI. Her receiving on her lap the sacred body of Jesus, taken down from the Cross. —One Our Father, seven Hail Marys.

VII. Her witnessing the burial of the sacred body of her Son.—One Our Father, seven Hail Marys.

In honour of the tears shed by our Lady during the Dolours.—Three Hail Marys.

Pray for us, O most sorrowful Virgin.

That we may be made worthy of the promises of Christ.

VENI, CREATOR.

[Proper before any undertaking.]

Veni, Creator Spiritus,
Mentes tuorum visita,
Imple superna gratia,
Quæ tu creasti pectora.

Qui diceris Paraclitus,
Altissimi donum Dei,
Fons vivus, ignis, charitas,
Et spiritalis unctio.

Tu septiformis munere,
Digitus Paternæ dexteræ,
Tu rite promissum Patris,
Sermone ditans guttura.

Accende lumen sensibus,
Infunde amorem cordibus,
Infirma nostri corporis
Virtute firmans perpeti.

Hostem repellas longius,
Pacemque dones protinus;
Ductore sic te prævio
Vitemus omne noxium.

Per te sciamus da Patrem,
Noscamus atque Filium,
Teque utriusque Spiritum
Credamus omni tempore.

VENI, CREATOR.

Come, O Creator Spirit blest!
And in our souls take up Thy rest;
Come, with Thy grace and heavenly aid,
To fill the hearts which Thou hast made.

Great Paraclete! to Thee we cry,
O highest gift of God most high!
O fount of life! O fire of love!
And sweet anointing from above!

Thou in Thy sevenfold gifts art known;
The finger of God's hand we own,
The promise of the Father Thou!
Who dost the tongue with power endow.

Kindle our senses from above,
And make our hearts o'erflow with love;
With patience firm, and virtue high,
The weakness of our flesh supply.

Far from us drive the foe we dread,
And grant us Thy true peace instead;
So shall we not, with Thee for guide,
Turn from the path of life aside.

Oh, may Thy grace on us bestow,
The Father and the Son to know,
And Thee through endless times confess'd
Of both th' Eternal Spirit blest.

Deo Patri sit gloria,
Et Filio, qui a mortuis
Surrexit, ac Paraclito,
In sæculorum sæcula.
                    Amen.

AVE MARIS STELLA.

Ave maris stella,
Dei Mater alma,
Atque semper Virgo,
Felix cœli porta.

Sumens illud Ave
Gabrielis ore,
Funda nos in pace,
Mutans Evæ nomen.

Solve vincla reis,
Profer lumen cæcis,
Mala nostra pelle,
Bona cuncta posce.

Monstra te esse matrem,
Sumat per te preces,
Qui pro nobis natus,
Tulit esse tuus.

All glory while the ages run
Be to the Father, and the Son
Who rose from death; the same to Thee,
O Holy Ghost eternally.   Amen.

100 *days'*; 300 *on Whit Sunday.*

AVE MARIS STELLA.

HAIL, thou star of ocean!
    Portal of the sky!
Ever Virgin Mother
    Of the Lord most high!

Oh! by Gabriel's Ave,
    Utter'd long ago,
Eva's name reversing,
    Grant us peace below.

Break the captive's fetters;
    Light on blindness pour;
All our ills expelling,
    Every bliss implore.

Show thyself a mother;
    Offer Him our sighs,
Who for us incarnate
    Did not thee despise.

Virgo singularis
Inter omnes mitis
Nos culpis solutos,
Mites fac et castos.

Vitam præsta puram,
Iter para tutum,
Ut videntes Jesum,
Semper collætemur.

Sit laus Deo Patri,
Summo Christo decus,
Spiritui Sancto,
Tribus honor unus.   Amen.

TE DEUM.

Te Deum laudamus * te Dominum confitemur.

Te æternum Patrem * omnis terra veneratur.

Tibi omnes angeli * tibi cœli et universæ potestates:

Tibi cherubim et seraphim * incessabili voce proclamant:

Sanctus, sanctus, sanctus, * Dominus Deus Sabaoth.

Virgin of all Virgins!
  To thy shelter take us:
Gentlest of the gentle!
  Chaste and gentle make us.

Still as on we journey,
  Help our weak endeavour;
Till with thee and Jesus
  We rejoice for ever.

Through the highest heaven,
  To the Almighty Three,
Father, Son, and Spirit,
  One same glory be.   Amen.

TE DEUM.

We praise Thee, O God: we acknowledge Thee to be the Lord.

All the earth doth worship Thee: the Father everlasting.

To Thee all Angels cry aloud: the Heavens and all the powers therein.

To Thee the Cherubim and Seraphim: continually do cry:

Holy, holy, holy: Lord God of Sabaoth.

Pleni sunt cœli et terra, * majestatis gloriæ tuæ.

Te gloriosus * Apostolorum chorus.

Te Prophetarum * laudabilis numerus.

Te Martyrum candidatus * laudat exercitus.

Te per orbem terrarum * sancta confitetur Ecclesia.

Patrem * immensæ majestatis.

Venerandum tuum verum * et unicum Filium.

Sanctum quoque * Paraclitum Spiritum.

Tu Rex gloriæ, * Christe.

Tu Patris * sempiternus es Filius.

Tu ad liberandum suscepturus hominem, * non horruisti Virginis uterum.

Tu devicto mortis aculeo, * aperuisti credentibus regna cœlorum.

Tu ad dexteram Dei sedes, * in gloria Patris.

Judex crederis * esse venturus.

Heaven and earth are full: of the majesty of Thy Glory.

The glorious choir of the Apostles: praise Thee.

The admirable company of the Prophets: praise Thee.

The white-robed army of Martyrs: praise Thee.

The Holy Church throughout all the world: doth acknowledge Thee.

The Father: of an infinite majesty.

Thy adorable, true: and only Son.

Also the Holy Ghost: the Comforter.

Thou art the King of Glory: O Christ.

Thou art the everlasting Son: of the Father.

When Thou tookest upon Thee to deliver man: Thou didst not abhor the Virgin's womb.

When Thou hadst overcome the sting of death: Thou didst open the kingdom of heaven to all believers.

Thou sittest at the right hand of God: in the glory of the Father.

We believe that Thou shalt come: to be our Judge.

† Te ergo quæsumus tuis famulis subveni, * quos pretioso sanguine redemisti.

Æterna fac cum Sanctis tuis, * in gloria numerari.

Salvum fac populum tuum, Domine, * et benedic hæreditati tuæ.

Et rege eos, et extolle illos, * usque in æternum.

Per singulos dies * benedicimus te.

Et laudamus nomen tuum in sæculum ;* et in sæculum sæculi.

Dignare, Domine, die isto, * sine peccato nos custodire.

Miserere nostri, Domine, * miserere nostri.

Fiat misericordia tua, Domine, super nos: quemadmodum speravimus in te.

In te Domine, speravi; * non confundar in æternum.

---

† Hic omnes genuflectuntur.

† We pray Thee, therefore, help Thy servants: whom Thou hast redeemed with Thy precious blood.

Make them to be numbered with Thy Saints: in glory everlasting.

O Lord, save Thy people: and bless Thine inheritance.

Govern them: and lift them up for ever.

Day by day: we magnify Thee.

And we praise Thy name for ever: yea, for ever and ever.

Vouchsafe, O Lord, this day: to keep us without sin.

O Lord, have mercy upon us: have mercy upon us.

O Lord, let Thy mercy be showed upon us: as we have hoped in Thee.

O Lord, in Thee have I hoped: let me not be confounded for ever.

---

† Here all kneel

www.ingramcontent.com/pod-product-compliance
Lightning Source LLC
Chambersburg PA
CBHW032135160426
43197CB00008B/654